THREE PADEREWSKI PLAYS

THREE PADEREWSKI PLAYS

BY KAZIMIERZ BRAUN

EDITED BY MAJA TROCHIMCZYK

MOONRISE PRESS

Copyright Information

Three Paderewski Plays by Kazimierz Braun, edited by Maja Trochimczyk is published by Moonrise Press. P.O. Box 4288, Los Angeles – Sunland, CA 91041-4288, www.moonrisepress.com.

Maestro Paderewski for one actor previously appeared in *Dramaty Zebrane. Collected Plays. Tom 1. Volume 1. Teatr Jednego Aktora. Plays For One Actor* by Kazimierz Braun (Moonrise Press, 2024).

Paderewski's Children and *Paderewski's Return* previously appeared in *Dramaty Zebrane. Collected Plays. Tom 4. Volume 4. Teatr Pamięci. Theater of Memory* by Kazimierz Braun (Moonrise Press, 2025).

© Copyright 2025 by Kazimierz Braun and Maja Trochimczyk

All Rights Reserved 2025 by Moonrise Press for this collection only.

Cover design by Maja Trochimczyk. Portrait of Paderewski in 1915, Public Domain. Fonts Brittanic Bold and Cambria.

No part of this book may be reproduced or utilized in any form or by any means, electronic or mechanical, including photocopying and recording, or by any information storage and retrieval system, without permission in writing from the author and publisher.

Manufactured in the United States of America

The Library of Congress Publication Data:

Kazimierz Braun (b. 1936), author and translator. Maja Trochimczyk (b. 1957), editor. [Three Paderewski Plays]

Three Paderewski Plays / Kazimierz Braun, author and translator / Maja Trochimczyk, editor.

196 pages (vi pp. prefatory matter, and 190 pp.); 6 in x 9 in. Written in English. With the author's introduction, and the editor's lists of Paderewski's writings and compositions, archives, and a bibliograpy.

ISBN 978-1-945938-84-9 (hardcover)
ISBN 978-1-945938-85-6 (paperback)
ISBN 978-1-945938-86-3 (eBook in ePub format)

10 9 8 7 6 5 4 3 2 1

THREE PADEREWSKI PLAYS

TABLE OF CONTENTS

Page 1
The Life and Work of Ignacy Jan Paderewski – By Kazimierz Braun

Page 19
Maestro Paderewski by Kazimierz Braun

Page 47
Paderewski's Children by Kazimierz Braun

Page 109
Paderewski's Return by Kazimierz Bran

Page 171
Paderewski's Writings by Maja Trochimczyk

Page 177
Paderewski's Compositions by Maja Trochimczyk

Page 184
Paderewski's Archives and Musea by Maja Trochimczyk

Page 185
Selected Books and Studies about Paderewski by Maja Trochimczyk

THE LIFE AND WORKS OF IGNACY JAN PADEREWSKI
by Kazimierz Braun

Figure 1: Photo of Paderewski from the early 1890s, taken in the studio of Jadwiga Golcz in Warsaw (National Digital Archives)

Paderewski is the pride of Poles. He is one of the three most important Polish activists and politicians who worked to achieve and win Poland's independence in 1918. These three great figures were Ignacy Jan Paderewski (1860-1941), Roman Dmowski (1864-1939), and Józef Piłsudski (1867-1935). Paderewski was deliberately forgotten by the ruling camp during the interwar period, and after the war, he was downright persecuted by the communists. Even today, much erroneous or incomplete information about him circulates online. To this day, there is no complete, objective monograph about him.

Ignacy Jan Paderewski had a unique & extraordinary personality. He profoundly and singularly influenced the history of Poland, the history of the Polish American community, the history of music, and the history of culture on a global scale. He was a pianist, composer, statesman, and philanthropist. Above all, he was a noble, generous, hard-working, and kind man. His contemporaries called him "immortal," but as an artist, he was undoubtedly a genius.

Who was Paderewski really? Who is he to us today? How can he help us live better? What was his vision of Poland? And what do we owe him? To answer these questions, we must first recall the most important facts about his life and work.

Ignacy Jan Paderewski's life is clearly divided into four periods.

The first period (1860-1888) encompasses twenty-eight years of study, preparation, his first public piano performances, and his first compositions.

The second period (1888-1915) spans over a quarter-century of a dazzling, global career of a piano virtuoso (ten concert tours in the U.S. and Canada, countess concerts in European cities, concert tours in South America, Australia and New Zealand), as well as a talented composer of original piano, chamber, and symphonic music, and an opera, *Manru*.

The third period (1915-1921) encompasses six years of active political activity. Paderewski assumed leadership of the Polish American community and advised U.S. President Wilson; served as President of the Council of Ministers and Minister of Foreign Affairs in Poland; represented Poland at the Versailles Peace

Conference and fulfilled his duties as the country's representative in various international bodies.

The fourth period (1922-1939), lasting seventeen years: a time of dominance on world stages as an iconic virtuoso pianist and globally recognized celebrity, and, at the same time, holding the position of the highest national authority.

Then, there was only a short epilogue to this long and beautiful life, the last two years (1939-1941) once again devoted entirely to public service—philanthropic activities and tireless advocacy for the Polish cause.

During the first period, Ignacy Jan Paderewski grew up in modest nobleman's manor houses in Podolia and Volhynia (his father Jan served as an administrator on country estates and moved occasionally). The youth did not know his mother, who orphaned him when he was just a few months old. At home, he received a basic general education, the basics of piano playing, and a patriotic formation: his father had been imprisoned by the Russians for a year for participating in the 1863 Uprising. Young Paderewski grew up in an atmosphere of remembrance of a great independent Poland, listening to stories of heroic victories and tragic uprisings, and feeling the burden—of Poland's captivity, enslaved by three partitioning powers Russia, Germany, and Austria for nearly a century.

At the age of 12, he began his musical education in Warsaw. His professors did not consider him particularly gifted, and one of them even advised him against continuing to play the piano. At eighteen, he graduated with excellent grades from the Warsaw Institute of Music (1878) and immediately thereafter took up piano teaching duties in the lower grades at the Institute. At the same time, he also started to compose, and soon after, created very mature works.

In January 1880, the young pianist married Antonina Korsak, a fellow student at the Warsaw Institute of Music, but his young wife died shortly after giving birth to their son, Alfred, in October 1880. The child, of very poor health, later also died young, undergoing treatment in Bavaria in 1901, on the same day as his father was giving a concert in Bilbao, Spain.

Meanwhile, the musician's career was boosted by the brilliant Polish actress Helena Modrzejewska (known in English as Modjeska, 1840-1909), to whom he was introduced during one of her returns from America for guest performances in Poland. Modjeska recognized Paderewski's immense talent and organized a benefit concert for him in Kraków (1884). The funds raised at this event, along with her own financial contribution, enabled Paderewski to study in Vienna (1885) with the renowned piano pedagogue Theodor Leschetizky (1830-1915); the studies were extended with a series of lessons two years later. Simultaneously, Paderewski worked tirelessly and constantly on himself.

His first concerts in Paris (1888), which ended in resounding success, paved the way for his rise to fame. Soon, the young pianist was performing in Belgium, Germany, England, Scotland, and finally in the United States (the first tour took place in 1891-92), gaining ever greater success, winning over critics and capturing the admiration of audiences. His phenomenal piano technique provided the unwavering foundation of his personal and innovative interpretations, crowned by inspired, ecstatic, and captivating playing. He was also a handsome, imposing man, and his golden, leonine mane gave him an extraordinary appearance and an aura of beauty. Since conquering the capitals of Europe and the great cities of America, Paderewski became a virtuoso of the highest international renown, the object of a cult known as "Paddymania." Furthermore, he commanded both respect and interest as a composer of music for piano, chamber ensembles, and symphony orchestra (Piano Concerto in A Major, Symphony in B Minor *Polonia*, and *Manru,* an opera inspired by a story by Józef Ignacy Kraszewski). The pianist-composer often played his own works in concerts, especially as encores. His most often performed encore was the *Minuet à l'Antique*, Opus 14, Number 1, composed in 1884.

While preparing for concerts, Paderewski rigorously practiced day and night, constantly imposing a ruthless schedule on himself. He often spent 17 hours a day at the piano, leaving four hours for sleep and three for meals. Hard work was the foundation of his success. Over the course of a quarter-century, he consistently reached the pinnacle of fame as a virtuoso, as well as social acclaim and financial success. He played at royal courts and presidential residences, was decorated with medals, and honored with honorary doctorates. He traveled the world, including ten grand tours of the United States and concert "expeditions" to South America, Australia, and New Zealand.

Over the years, the successful pianist-composer did not forget his "landed gentry" roots and productive life on country estates. He purchased an estate in Kąśna Dolna near Tarnów, two ranches in California near Paso Robles, and a large mansion in Riond-Bosson, near Morges in Switzerland. Being enormously generous, he donated vast sums to charities, scholarships, foundations, and a whole array of charitable causes. This chord of his activity resonated powerfully when he founded the Grunwald Monument in Kraków, marking the 500th anniversary of the victorious battle of joint Polish and Lithuanian troops against the Teutonic Knights (1910). It was a great national act, which for the first time revealed Paderewski the virtuoso and composer to Poland, and to its troubled partitioning powers—as a passionate orator, a steadfast patriot, and a charismatic leader, capable of capturing the hearts and imaginations of the masses.

Figure 2: Villa owned by Ignacy Paderewski in Riond-Bosson near Morges in Switzerland. (National Museum, Warsaw).

By founding the Grunwald Monument in Kraków, gathering crowds for its unveiling, and addressing them, Paderewski evoked the nation's glorious past and focused its hopes for a better future, for independence. He reiterated this message in a speech at the centenary celebrations of Chopin's birth in Lwów (1910). He increasingly empathized with the suffering of Poles at home and established ever closer contacts with the Polish diaspora in America. Poles around the world were proud of him and gradually promoted him to a leadership position. In the following years, Paderewski resumed a demanding regimen of frequent concerts, requiring virtually constant travel.

During World War I, Paderewski, first in Switzerland and then in the U.S., undertook enormous and energetic charitable and political projects, working on several fronts simultaneously. At this time, he conducted intensive, highly detailed, self-taught studies of Polish history and geography, which prepared him for the greatest task he was undertaking—ensuring that Poland regains independence. In particular:

(1) The pianist helped Poles materially: he created the Polish Victims' Relief Fund (co-chaired with Nobel Prize winner, writer Henryk Sienkiewicz, with headquarters in Switzerland and chapters in the U.K., France, and the U.S.), collecting money for its charitable programs and directing his earnings to it. In this way, he helped Poles in a country devastated by the shifting fronts and battles of German, Russian, and Austrian troops.

(2) He engaged in political activities aimed at resurrecting an independent Polish state: he joined the Polish National Committee (Komitet Narodowy Polski, KNP), established in Paris by Roman Dmowski, as its member and delegate to the United States. The KNP was the seed of the Polish government abroad and was later recognized as such by the Allies (1917).

(3) He commenced efforts to unite all Polish organizations in the United States, which he almost completely succeeded in doing, and thanks to which Polonia spoke with one voice on matters concerning their homeland. Paderewski himself became the informal leader of the entire Polish American community.

(4) The pianist launched a broad information and advocacy campaign on behalf of Poland in the United States, conducted on

two levels simultaneously. On the one hand, he appealed to American public opinion and mobilized it on behalf of Poland. For this purpose, he devised an unusual method, unique to himself: a piano concert combined with a political rally. First, he played the piano (mostly music by Fryderyk Chopin), drawing thousands under his name as a world-renowned virtuoso. Then, he rose from the piano and delivered a vibrant speech on the need to revive an independent Poland and assist Polish war victims, caught in the crossfire of battles they did not start. In three years, Paderewski gave over three hundred such concert-rallies. On the other hand, the patriotic pianist established cooperation with the American government and President Woodrow Wilson (1856-1924, serving in 1913-1921), whom he met personally. At the President's request, Paderewski prepared a memorandum on Polish affairs, outlining the reasons why Poland must regain its independence and demonstrating its appropriate borders, with access to the Baltic Sea.

Thanks to Paderewski, and based on his memorandum, President Wilson incorporated the famous Point 13 into his peace program, which stipulated, as a condition for post-war peace, a united, independent Poland, within just borders, with access to the sea (January 1918). It was this memorandum by Paderewski, and Wilson's postulate based on it, that brought the Polish cause into the orbit of the war goals and post-war objectives of the coalition countries fighting against Germany and Austro-Hungary—the United States of America, Great Britain, France, and later Italy. These countries identified Poland's regained independence as an important element of the post-war world order.

(5) In the spring of 1916, Paderewski proposed (based on earlier Polish efforts in France) the creation of a Polish Army fighting alongside the United States. After various delays, such an army began to form in the autumn of 1916, and was formally created on October 6, 1917. It reached a strength of over 22,000 soldiers. All of them were volunteers from Polish immigrant families. This was Paderewski's army. France provided its blue uniforms and weapons. Hence, it was called the "Blue Army." Training took place in Canada, a dominion of Great Britain, which was fighting Germany. (The USA did not formally participate in the war until April 6, 1917.)

Figure 3: Head of State Józef Piłsudski (first from the left), Prime Minister Ignacy Jan Paderewski (middle), Minister of Internal Affairs Stanisław Wojciechowski (behind Paderewski) and Piłsudski's assistant, lieutenant Tadeusz Kasprzycki (first from the right) after a solemn service in the St. John Cathedral, Warsaw, February 9, 1919 (National Digital Archives).

In May 1918, this army was transferred to France and immediately entered combat. Its political leadership was secured by Roman Dmowski's Paris-based Polish National Committee, which appointed General Józef Haller (1873-1960) as its commander on October 4, 1918. From that date, the "Blue Army" also began to be called "Haller's Army," or "Hallerczyks." This army absorbed more Poles—Allied prisoners of war and deserters from the occupying powers' armies—and grew to approximately 80,000, ensuring Poland's participation in the Allied victory parade in Paris in November 1918. It was then used to decisively reinforce the forces of the reborn homeland.

All this work and its visible fruits naturally designated the pianist and patriot for his next, most important task: assuming leadership of all Poles, beyond the partitioned borders and party differences, uniting all the best Polish forces in the country and around the world. Therefore, Paderewski decided to return to Warsaw, an undertaking facilitated by the Allies.

After landing on an English warship in Gdańsk on December 25, 1918, Paderewski arrived the very next day, December 26, in Poznań, where his mere appearance sparked an uprising and, consequently, the annexation of a vast part of the Prussian partition to the Polish-Lithuanian Commonwealth. On January 1, 1919, Paderewski arrived in Warsaw. He was greeted as a savior. This welcome was even more enthusiastic than that of Józef

Piłsudski after his return from a German prison six weeks earlier. Paderewski, besides his legendary status as a world-renowned musician, a passionate patriot, and a generous philanthropist, brought with him military and financial support of the Allies. He announced the return to his homeland of a select army, currently concentrated in France; the transfer of Western funds and economic aid to Poland; as well as the assurance of peace within broad secure borders, encompassing vast areas of the former Polish-Lithuanian Commonwealth. He had a triple mandate behind him: the will of the majority of Poles at home and abroad, the authorization of the Paris-based Polish National Committee, and the support of the victorious Allies.

However, in Warsaw, Józef Piłsudski, raised to power by popular will and hope, was already in power. He held the office of the Chief of State ("Naczelnik Państwa"—so dubbed in imitation of Thadeus Kościuszko, the leader of insurrection against the 2nd partition of Poland by its hostile neighbors in 1794) and patronized the socialist government of Jędrzej Moraczewski (1870-1944). Piłsudski initially refused to share power with Paderewski. However, he soon realistically assessed Paderewski's personal value and the political "dowry" he offered. On January 16, 1919, Piłsudski appointed him as the President of the Council of Ministers and, simultaneously, the Minister of Foreign Affairs.

As the head of Polish government, Paderewski undertook the monumental task of organizing the laws, administrative systems, and economy of the "resurrected" country. Above all, he focused on unifying the lands and populations of the three former partitions, with distinct traditions, rules, and institutions created and implemented over the course of 123 years by the three occupying powers, Russia, Prussia and Austria.

He then participated in the Versailles Peace Conference, where Roman Dmowski had previously served as Poland's delegate. Paderewski recognized Dmowski's leadership position in the Paris-based Polish National Committee and his enormous diplomatic contribution to regaining and strengthening Poland's independence, while Dmowski wisely understood the immense personal authority of Paderewski and the capital of the trust he enjoyed among the Western Allies. Dmowski therefore loyally gave Paderewski the position of First Polish Delegate at the Peace Conference, becoming the Second Delegate himself.

There was something captivating, extraordinary, symbolic, and downright mystical about the fact that a resurrected Poland was represented at the World Peace Conference by a great musician; everyone knew that as an artist, he stood at the top. But the political struggle that raged throughout the Conference was dominated by something else: his unique, powerful personality, inextricably intertwined with iron will and delicate sensitivity; his organized historical knowledge with the creative inspiration of a speaker; his gift for establishing personal rapport, openness to his interlocutor, and seeking common ground with them, combined with the ability to maintain his own opinion. All of this was grounded in fanatical diligence, refined culture, and impeccable manners, and supported by his knowledge of many languages, as well as European and Polish history, geography, and economic issues. For representatives of major powers and small nations, Paderewski maintained respect and communicated with them on the level of universal values, the common good, and universal justice. He often clashed with the other side's different value system, with ruthlessness and political cynicism, with the interests of the stronger imposed by force on the weaker. But he stood his ground.

At the Versailles Peace Conference, Paderewski and Dmowski won everything they could for Poland, undoubtedly more than anyone else could have. For themselves, it was not enough, but they understood the implications of the decisions made.

During the Conference, Paderewski led efforts to transport "his" Blue Army home. Despite obstacles placed in his way by Germany and England, he succeeded in having the Blue Army, under the command of General Haller, transferred to the now-independent Poland. Its soldiers became a key force in the war against the Bolsheviks in 1920, repelling the invasion by the Red Army that suffered a stunning defeat during the Battle of Warsaw.

Upon returning to Warsaw from the Versailles Peace Conference in July 1919, Paderewski was unjustly accused of yielding to the Allies. He gradually lost support—both from Piłsudski and from political parties. He was distrusted by Wincenty Witos (1874-1945), a popular leader who, having spent years molding himself in the Austrian parliament, did not understand Paderewski's non-partisan position and political style, nor his program of uniting national forces beyond all divisions and particularisms. Roman Dmowski remained loyal, but was far away, in Paris. Polish hell opened before Paderewski. On December 10, 1919, he resigned from his posts. In February 1920, he left the country for Switzerland, making Riond-Bosson his home. He would never return to Warsaw. However, when the Bolsheviks arrived at the capital's gates in 1920, Paderewski once again declared his readiness to serve Poland. He accepted the position of Polish delegate to the Council of Ambassadors and the League of Nations in Geneva. He fought for Poland as a diplomat.

Figure 4: Ignacy Jan Paderewski among those welcoming him on December 27, 1918 in Poznań. (National Digital Archives).

After Poland won the war, with great impact of the "Blue Army," Paderewski was no longer needed by the government. The soldiers, after making vital contributions to the victory over the Red Army, were not needed either and gradually returned to the U.S., penniless and displaced from their pre-war, stable lives.

Having ended his political career, Paderewski decided to return to the concert stage. In early 1921, he left for America and stayed for six months in Paso Robles, California, where he owned vineyards, two ranches, and had access to hot springs. Before his return to the career of virtuoso pianist, he imposed on himself a grueling practice schedule, refreshing his technique and mastering the repertoire. He was already 61 years old.

Paderewski's first performance in years at the Carnegie Hall in New York (November 22, 1922) is described as one of the greatest events in the history of 20th-century music. Perhaps the greatest? A widely known and respected statesman appeared on stage. The hall honored him with a standing ovation. Then, the great virtuoso gave a concert, playing with absolute perfection. The audience, the music world, fellow artists, critics, and impresarios were enchanted, delighted, and captivated.

Thus, Paderewski returned to the stage and for the next dozen or so years reigned supreme, touring extensively. He made many recordings that documented his technique and musicality. The virtuoso spent his rest periods in Switzerland.

In this period, he came to be called "the immortal." Indeed, a book titled *Paderewski, The Story of a Modern Immortal* by Charles Phillips was published in New York in 1933. This title and the overwhelming and universal adoration by his audiences were inspired not only by his musical genius, but also by his unparalleled generosity—thousands benefitted from his charitable donations to scholarships, schools, hospitals, veterans' unions, homeless shelters, and more.

Alas, since 1920, a veil of silence had been drawn over Paderewski in Poland—not in America. He was treated by the government as a—still potential—rival for power and was therefore kept away from the country. The chasm deepened when, in the second half of the 1930s, after the death of Marshal Piłsudski, Paderewski patronized the efforts of General Władysław Sikorski (1881-1943), General Józef Haller, and Wincenty Witos (by then not only deprived of influence but also persecuted), who advanced a program to heal Polish politics, forming with Paderewski the so-called Front Morges (1936).

In this period, he lived his life as a *de facto* exiled statesman and still active virtuoso. Only occasionally did news of his successes reach Poland. In 1937, the *Moonlight Sonata*, an English film starring Paderewski, was screened in Poland. This rare production was made all the more special that the Maestro played a whole 20-minute recital, filmed in its entirety!

He eagerly shared his skills and knowledge with younger musicians, inviting a select group to training sessions at his Swiss residence in Riond-Bosson. Finally, the pianist curated a monumental complete edition of Chopin's works edited by music historian Ludwik Bronarski (1890-1975) and pianist Józef Turczyński (1884-1953), drawing from Chopin's original manuscripts, first editions, and approved copies. Still in print, this is the most popular edition of Chopin's music in the world.

Figure 5: Composer and pianist Ignacy Jan Paderewski with wife Helena Paderewska (third and fourth from the right) during a visit to the Prime Minister of France, Raymond Poincaré with wife Henriette (first and second from the right), 1919 (National Digital Archives).

The lost war with Germany and the Soviet invasion of Poland in 1939 once again created the need to appeal to Paderewski's authority. Being already 79 years old, with his strength greatly diminished, Paderewski declined the offer of the office of President of Poland. However, he did not shirk the chairmanship of the National Council of the Republic of Poland in Paris in 1940. Soon, as a national emissary, he traveled to the United States to mobilize American, world, and Polish diaspora opinion on behalf of Poland.

He died there in 1941, after a difficult year filled with a grueling program of travel, talks, conferences, and speeches. By President Roosevelt's personal decision, Paderewski was buried with the highest state honors America can offer a head of state at Arlington National Cemetery in Washington DC.

Unfortunately, for the second time, the post-war communist government drew a curtain of silence over Paderewski, or rather, over his memory. He had inscribed himself on pages of Polish history that the communists had ripped from textbooks and tried to tear from the hearts of Poles. Therefore, it was forbidden to speak of his crucial role in the resurrection of Poland. Paderewski could only be spoken of as a musician—and as little as possible. While his compositional talent was nearly completely ignored by music historians, even his pianistic achievements were dismissed as due to his popularity, without true artistic merit.

Paderewski's memory was also inconvenient for the communists because its main bearer was Sylwin Strakacz (1892-1973), his former secretary and an emigrant living in California. For over 30 years, he served Paderewski with absolute loyalty and complete devotion, accompanying him on his travels, representing him in Poland, and collaborating politically abroad. Strakacz was a man of impeccable character and pristine reputation. During the Second World War, he earned the respect and love of the Polish American community by serving as the Consul General of the Republic of Poland (i.e. its Government-in-Exile) in New York.

After the war, and the installation of the Polish People's Republic's representatives in the Consulate, replacing those from the Polish Government-in-Exile in London, Strakacz was removed from office. Nonetheless, he faithfully continued to defend Paderewski's good name, his last will, and the remnants of his estate against the communist authorities. The continued attacks on Strakacz also besmirched Paderewski's memory. Only for the Polish American community was Paderewski a source of constant pride. His heart, designated to the care of American Polonia by his last will, was hidden in hospital vaults for decades until 1986, when it was ceremonially transferred to the National Shrine of Our Lady of Częstochowa in Doylestown, Pennsylvania. It remains there until today, staying with his most dedicated Polish-American constituency, just like Chopin's heart rests in Warsaw.

Only political changes in Poland, putting an end to the Polish People's Republic in 1989, allowed Paderewski's remains to return to Poland. In 1992, the ashes of the Great Pole were brought to Warsaw from the Arlington Cemetery and solemnly interred in the crypt of the St. John's Cathedral, where Mazovian princes and state leaders are buried.

In 2001, the Polish Parliament (Seym) passed a resolution to commemorate the 60th anniversary of Paderewski's death in a special way. Then, in 2018, on the occasion of the centennial of the restoration of Poland's independence, his contributions to this cause were celebrated worldwide with conferences, exhibitions, concerts, and more.

Paderewski's life was a source of encouragement and hope for millions of Poles, a model of integrity and patriotism, as well as of personal diligence and selfless public service. Before the Polish Pope, John Paul II, Paderewski was the most well-known and respected Pole in the world.

In Poland ruled by the Polish United Workers' Party (PZPR) and controlled by their handlers from Soviet Union, for many years, Paderewski was the focus of love for millions of Poles and hatred for the political elite. For many, he was a great statesman. For others, especially from the Piłsudski camp, he was an ineffective politician. For pianists, music lovers, and connoisseurs, he was a master of the piano and a great composer. For professional music historians, though—a somewhat dubious celebrity, too famous to be truly good… Gradually, over time, his memory faded. Only the Polish diaspora in America has always remembered him vividly. During three decades after the war, a Paderewski Foundation was giving out scholarships and prizes. In 1993, a Paderewski Festival was established in Paso Robles, followed by the initiation of a Paderewski Lecture-Recital series at the University of Southern California in 2002, the formation of the Paderewski Music Society in Los Angeles in 2008, and the creation of another Paderewski Festival in Raleigh, North Carolina in 2014.

In modern Poland – once again independent – it is good to remember Ignacy Jan Paderewski, who played a decisive role in restoring the country's independence a century ago. We can constantly return to Paderewski with pride and gratitude – for strength and inspiration. It is our noble, national duty to do justice to Ignacy Paderewski.

Figure 6: Ignacy Jan Paderewski in one of the film scenes in Moonlight Sonata in 1937, the film included a 20-minute recital by the pianist (National Digital Archives).

Much work as to be done by Polish scholars and historians to restore his reputation as an influential and visionary statesman, a great, innovative composer—who brought Wagnerian music drama, Debussy-stye impressionism, and stylized Tatra-mountain folk melodies into Polish music, and a iconic, global celebrity pianist of profound musica insights and incredible technical prowess. After Poland fully embraces his achievements and honors his contributions, Paderewski's name will be restored to his rightful pace in the world history.

Kazimierz Braun

THREE PADEREWSKI PLAYS

BY KAZIMIERZ BRAUN

MAESTRO PADEREWSKI

NOTES

Music. Music is required in the presentation of this drama. Specific oeuvres by Fryderyk Chopin and Ignacy Paderewski are indicated in the text. They can be produced mechanically—in full synchronization with the action. Sound effects are also needed.

Space. Action takes place in the chamber at the Warsaw's Royal Castle—the office of the President of the Council of Ministers in 1919, and in the places called up in the imagination of Ignacy Paderewski. There is a desk—on which papers, a telephone, fountain pens. Behind the desk an armchair, in front of the desk a stool—as for playing the piano.

Props. An essential prop is a large map of Poland within the borders of 1772. It should be at least 2x2 meters in size. At some point of the action, it is shown on the stage then removed. Also: a box in which a bottle of wine "Paderewski Zinfandel" (or more bottles) and a few (or more) glasses.

≡ ♫ ≡

Ignacy Paderewski enters—in the narrow spotlight. He is dressed as for a concert—in a tailcoat and white shirt with a white bow tie. He bows to the audience. There is a storm of applause. Paderewski sits down on a stool, three-quarters back to the audience, as if he were sitting down at a piano—which is not there—only a little further there is the desk. He raises his hands and strikes the non-existent keyboard.

♪ He begins Chopin's "Revolutionary Etude". He plays only the first three phrases, then he stops the movement of his fingers, but the music continues— while he turns to the audience and speaks:

IGNACY PADEREWSKI: A scream! Lamentation! Chopin's *Revolutionary Etude* begins with a scream. A terrible scream! This scream falls in cascades of chords into an abyss of despair, pain, protest, dissent from injustice, discontent for enslavement. Ah, how many times have I played that masterful oeuvre. How many times have I fallen with this music, like with the cascades of a great waterfall into this deathless abyss.

♪ The music continues.

Paderewski stands up and continues speaking directly to the audience.
    The left hand—and the left hand is the foundation of this work— with horror sweeps some debris, ruins, burned rubble; it runs back and forth through some barely cold battlefields, again, and again, and again. The right hand wants to fight, but it collapses under the onslaught of waves of lamentations, assaults of suffering, strokes of pain which every now and then fall on it from a sky-high height, pushing it to the very bottom of the dark abyss.
    Both hands make a brief attempt to calm down, to silence, to forget. In vain! The left hand is unable to break its run through the dark labyrinths. The right hand screams again tearfully, no longer singing, no longer touching the keys, but pounding on the bare strings, struggling, as if it wanted to smash, shatter the keyboard, the whole piano, break the prison bars closing on all sides.
    The struggle continues. A storm of sound is raging. The right hand seems to be catching up with the left hand; it leaves it alone for a moment in its terrible rush; it levels a breathless run with it. No! There is no agreement. There is revolt! There is no consolation. There is protest! There is defiance. There is no solace. There's despair. So, the melody sinks into the meltdown of hopelessness, overwhelmed by darkness.
    Only for a moment hope dawns for the victory of light over darkness, like a ray of sunshine suddenly ejaculating from

among the storm clouds. But it is only for a moment. Hope is again consumed by dark pain.
♪ *The music ends and wild applause erupts.*

Paderewski acknowledges it with taking bows. The applause lasts for a long time – against its backdrop Paderewski speaks:
    That was... It has been said of me that music sings through my hands... That I am a piano wizard, a piano poet, that I play the piano as if a whole symphony orchestra sounded.

♪ *The applause gradually ceases.*

    Indeed, I have worked out—indeed, it was a work, an extremely hard work—but I have worked it out, practicing for hours, days, years—my own method, known only to me, which no one else has ever managed to achieve.
    Lo and behold! When my right hand played one melody and my left hand played another, then—by speeding up or retarding by an infinite tiny fraction of a second the tempo of one hand or the other—I was able to play both melodies separately, but at the same time either combine them, or divide them. This was my famous "Tempo rubato", which gave my playing this great melodic richness, giving the impression of a whole orchestra.
    And I was said to be a genius. The old Camille Saint-Saëns, joked: "Mr. Paderewski is a genius who, in addition, plays the piano..." I was compared to Prospero, who wields both spirits and nature. Or, it was written that in my playing there is the dramatic wandering of Odysseus through storms and perils, and then the calm waves of the safe harbor of Ithaca. Suddenly Promethean torrents of fire fly through the piano and Zeus' thunder gushes from it.... What was admired in my music was the unusual combination of intellectualism and emotionality, the juxtaposition of pianissimo whispering with titanic striking power....
That was.
    I lived in the world of music. In its palace. In its royal residence. As its householder, then host, soon master. Then the ruler.

I was called the "Lion of Paris" because I sometimes threw myself at the piano with such force as if I wanted to devour it, destroy it, drive it into the ground. Or, suddenly, I lifted it lightly, lightly, like a feather, to glide with it among the stars.

That first concert of mine in Paris.... The year was 1888, I was 28 years old, 24 of them at the keyboard—for I was seated at it in our manor house in Polish Podolia when I was four years old. When I was twelve I was sent to the Conservatory of Music in Warsaw. Then there were years of study under eminent pedagogues in Vienna, Berlin. And hours, days and nights of my own incessant work. The lava was accumulating, as in a volcano. It erupted at this concert in Paris.

London received me coldly, and then ignited with the warmest enthusiasm. Soon I was touring all over Europe. Trains. Trains. Trains. A separate carriage-lounge, of course. Between concerts, I practiced constantly, several hours a day. In periods just before concerts, even seventeen hours at the keyboard. Four for sleep. Three for meals and rest. And again—the keyboard. To achieve perfection. And to surpass perfection by inspiration. Concerts. The crowds. Applause. Applause. Concerts. The crowds. Applause. Applause.

I took a trip to America. Ocean. Piano in the lounge on the ship—and there practice, practice, practice. Ah, how that trip gets so long. But I used every second of it to refine the perfection of my fingers. So let the sailing continue. Until the fingers become absolutely fit.

Ten concerts in America. Thirty concerts in America. One hundred concerts in America. First tour all over the United States in 1891, second one a year later, then another, and another – until ten have accumulated so far. Still on the road. Trains, automobiles, stagecoaches, carriages. Everywhere my Steinway grand piano had to be taken. I myself supervised its transportation from the train station as well as tuning. I sat down to practice on it before the concert. I practiced constantly.

Concert halls, ballrooms, movie theaters, theaters' stages. Applause. Applause. Applause. Honoraria. Honoraria fabulous. And again, Europe, Europe. Europe. Concerts. Applause. Exercises. Concerts. Applause. Exercises. Concerts. Applause. Applause. Mad applause.

I've played for the crowds, and I played in royal courts, in the residences of presidents, in the palaces of aristocrats, in the salons of female admirers. Applause. Applause. Applause.

I ventured out to the Antipodes. Seas. Oceans. Seas. Oceans. Oceans. I gained wild success in Australia and in New Zealand. Again applause. Applause. Applause.

Shoals of flying fish swooping down in front of the ship's bow. Shoals of money. Shoals of flattering reviews. And Europe again, including, finally Poland—Warsaw, then, Kraków, then Lwów. Crowds again. Applause. Applause. Applause. The joy and pride of my countrymen. I played them Chopin most often, ah, each time lamenting the enslavement of the homeland in the *Revolutionary Etude*....

♪ *He listens—and we hear for a moment— again— the beginning of the "Revolutionary Etude."*

I performed Liszt's *Second Hungarian Rhapsody*, my favorite. Beethoven's *Moonlight Sonata*. I played both Schubert and Wagner. And, of course, my own compositions. How many times, with what great conductors, have I played my *Piano Concerto in A minor, Opus 17*.

♪ *He listens—and we hear— the beginning of this "Concerto", including the first bars of the piano solo.*

The orchestra begins with a great collective beat. Soon from the torrent of sounds the violins emerge and dominate for a moment, as if carried by a great wave; then flutes, violas, cellos, trumpets, rumbling drums, once again a great tutti—which quiets down and introduces gently the singing of the piano....

I was also very fond of playing my *Polish Fantasy in G-sharp Minor, Opus 19*— by its very title, reminding listeners of my beautiful but unhappy country....

♪ *He listens—and we hear—the beginning of the "Polish Fantasy": orchestra—piano—orchestra.*

This piece also begins with a majestic grand orchestra. It is shortly joined and, as it were, punctuated, by a ceremonial entrance by the piano—the piano that immediately becomes independent and erupts in cascades of frenzied, free-flowing chords climbing to sky-high heights. And there, the orchestra is waiting for the piano with all its might, as it would like to devour it, but the piano sneaks out, regains its freedom, and dominates again... It is Poland that gathers its power, extracts it from the depths of its being, and then announces its will extract itself to freedom. Intertwined are two themes—collective power and the relentless drive for liberty....

Ah, after all, there was also my great Symphony in B-minor, Polonia.

♪ *He listens—and we hear—the beginning of the "Symphony Polonia in B-minor."*

In this music it's as if I'm slowly opening up the ever-widening horizons of our beautiful country—planes of fertile fields, ranges of lofty mountains, walls of majestic forests, oh, here light mists are rising from above the meadows, and there the plow is already putting away the sods of black soil....

And there were my Polish dances—folk dances, my Tatra rhythms, and court dances—my *Polonaises*... I composed about Poland. I composed Poland... I resurrected the still enslaved Poland with my music...

I also smuggled my old youthful but already mature pieces into the repertoires—for contrast, to catch my breath, to cheer up the audience and make fun of myself. Ah, how I liked this little *Humoresque Opus 14*....

He sits down on the stool—as at the beginning—in front of a non-existent piano.
♪ *He begins to play "Humoresque Opus 14."*

After the first three bars, he stops moving his fingers, turns to the audience, speaks—maybe he will stand up to be closer to the audience, or even he will sit on the edge of the forestage, as telling the spectators a fairy tale—while the music continues to be heard.

The rhythm is expressive from the start. Allegretto. But first it sings, as if testing it tentatively, as if carefully wrapping the rhythm with melody. Well. There is the rhythm. There is the melody. There is singing. There is harmony. So now boldly, vigorously—once again and once again. Rhythm laced with melody. Melody guided by rhythm. I'm dancing an old-fashioned dance with my fingers, and all around me swirl the shadows of Bach, Mozart, Beethoven, who wrote such kind of compositions in which they seemed to rest, to simply enjoy themselves, to forget about the whole world but music—just like me, just like me.

You can dance this piece en deux, you can dance en troi, so, paired with your beloved, or with two lovers, at two sides, one—a bass lover, the other—a violin lover. And once again that rhythm and singing. And again.

Ah, I've had enough of the wedge of this rhythm, I'll break! A moment of madness, a run that no one can catch up with, a display of my incredible technique, an explosion of titanic energy.

And I'm again slowing down, overwhelmed by nostalgia. I abscond from the dancers, I leave the ballroom through the wide-open door, I stand on the terrace of a manor and the vast, barely pink sky of dawn opens before me. Longing pulls me into some abyssal distance. Should I go there? No. I won't. I tread softly back into the ballroom.

Again, I throw myself into the vortex of dancing madly, hurriedly, loudly. Again, I slow down. Again, I dance faster. Legs—a tiny step, on tiptoes. Right hand—given to the lady on my right. Left hand—given to the lady on my left. Bow. Passing two hands. Bow. Passing two hands. Joined. Jointed. Joint rotation. Joint rotation. Bowing.

From the rocking waves of the slippery dance floor, I return suddenly to the safe haven of the piano. I dance with light fingers. I take a moment to joke, smile, and banter, run somewhere, come back from somewhere. The right hand suddenly wants to escape the keyboard at all by running toward the farthest keys, producing the highest, pearly tones. The right hand brings it back.

They are both dancing again. I am dancing. I'm not just dancing with one or two ladies, I'm dancing with all the most beautiful women in the world, I'm twirling, and more, and more. Chord. The finale. The end.

♪ *Again, the applause rings out.*

One morning, after returning to Switzerland from another tour, bringing again baskets of laudatory reviews and bags of earned money, I stepped out onto the balcony of my palace to watch the rising sun painting in pink the snows of the Mont Blanc. In front of me was the calm depths of the Lake Geneva. An absolutely smooth mirror of water.

Behind it the huge mountain. Uplifted so high as to defy the sky. The power of eternal nature confronts me. Awe and humility. But it is I who create with my eyes both the mountain and the lake, I create them with my gaze. When I close my eyes they disappear. When I open—I call them out of non-existence. My power of the creator.

I gazed into the water of the lake. And suddenly I saw a huge edifice sunk in it. No, there was a whole vast country submerged. Horror. This country was emerging from the depths and could not come to the surface. Although it was in the water, fires were creeping there, burned ruins were smoking, houses were crumbling. My compatriots wandered there. They all had shackles on their hands and legs. Along the roads foreign armies were marching and prowling. This was my homeland. This was Poland. Plunged into deep waters of slavery.

The vision was so strong that for a long time I could not tear myself away from it. Finally, I closed the door of the balcony with a slam. But the vision stayed with me. I realized that I must bring my country out of the slavery. Make my nation free again. Resurrect it. Resurrect Poland.

No longer just playing about it. No longer just inserting it into the notes of my compositions. I must rebuild the great edifice of my country in its actual, real, material being. I have to determine its borders. I have to re-erect demolished houses, furnish them. I have to feed the hungry. I set about this great work.

Paderewski takes off his tailcoat, which he hangs somewhere, and puts on his black frock coat.

Stone by stone. Brick by brick. Beam by beam. Rafter by rafter. First, I erected in Kraków the monument of the great Polish victory over the Teutonic Knights at Grunwald on the 500th anniversary of the memorable, victorious battle of 1410.

Paderewski speaks to the crowds at the unveiling of the Grunwald Monument in Krakow in 1910:

"Compatriots! The monument we are looking at was not born out of hatred. It was born of a deep love of the Motherland, not only in its past greatness and present incapacity, but also in its bright, strong future. It was born out of love and gratitude for those of our ancestors who did not go to the battlefields for loot, not for conquest, but in defense of a just and good cause they took up arms victoriously. Let every Pole from each of the former lands of Poland, or from across the Ocean, look to this monument as a sign of a common past, a testimony of shared glory, and an encouragement to join in a fruitful work for the future. May all the children of this soil be inspired by love and harmony, filled with the serenity of hope and the power of faith in the resurrection of Poland, our mother!"

My words were listened by the terrified foreigners ruling in Poland. And when the Great War broke out and they threw themselves at each other's throats I sensed that the moment of history had arrived.

With a quick step he unrolls or introduces on the stage a big map. We see the map of Poland from 1772. On the map are clearly drawn the borders of the country, the biggest cities – Warsaw, Kraków, Poznań, Gdańsk, Wilno, Lwów; the names of neighboring countries: Russia, Austria, Prussia. At the top of the map, we see the inscription: The Republic of Poland in 1772.

THE REPUBLIC OF POLAND, 1772

Paderewski turns to President Wilson sitting—in his imagination —behind the desk.

This, Mister President, is a map of my homeland, Poland. It was like this in 1772. Then, in successive waves of three partitions, it began to be invaded, conquered, until finally annihilated, by three evil neighbors—Russia, Prussia, and Austria. But this Poland is there. It lives in the hearts of all Poles. There, overseas, in these vast lands, and here, in America, in the hearts of Polish immigrants. And you, Mr. President, you have the power to resurrect this Poland.

To the audience:
American President Woodrow Wilson listened to me attentively. He asked me to present him with a detailed memorandum describing the history, geography, and population composition of my country.

In a hurry, Paderewski brings a thick portfolio of documents from a corner of the stage. He sits down on the stool facing the desk. He says:
Dear and Respectable Mister President, in the interest of humanity, for the sake of liberty and justice, the Polish problem must be solved by the reconstruction of the entire Polish state, by the liberation of the Polish nation...

He shows on a map what he is talking about. He speaks either to the—imagined—President Wilson, or to the audience.
I wrote an extensive memorandum for President Wilson. I gave him exact figures for all Polish provinces in terms of the territories, population, and even faith of the inhabitants.

All this is the Polish land, Mister President. A Republic of Two Nations. Poland and Lithuania.

Starting from the west, Mister President, here is the Grand Duchy of Posen, the ancient cradle of our nation. The land seized by Prussia. The territory of the Grand Duchy of Posen covers 28,996 square kilometers. It has two million one hundred thousand inhabitants, of which 67.7% are Catholics, 30.79% Protestants, 1.26%, Jews. The Polish population, the most numerous, is one million two hundred and ninety-one thousand.

I moved to describing in detail Western and Eastern Prussia, and Silesia.

Now, this is the heart of our nation, Mister President, this is The Kingdom of Poland. Territory 127,684 square kilometers. 12,476,000 population. Of which 75% Poles, 3% Lithuanians, 2.7% Ruthenians, 1.1% Russians, 14.6 Jews, 4% Germans. More than 80% Catholic.

Next goes the Grand Duchy of Lithuania with its two million indigenous inhabitants... I have discussed in detail both the lands and population of Lithuania. I moved on to Belarus. And then I spoke about the Austrian partition, with its nearly five million Polish, Catholic population.

All this is Poland, Mister President. Great Poland. It should be resurrected!

Thus, I presented President Wilson with a detailed plan for the resurrection of Poland, the reestablishment of Poland. He listened. I convinced him! He accepted my plan as his own. He declared the resurrection of Poland, and that with access to the Baltic sea, as one of the goals of the war.

Paderewski takes down the map.

I won the American government for the Polish cause! I ignited the hearts of the four-million-strong Polish American community for the Polish cause.

I devised a way to reach those Polish masses in America. I announced a concert with free admission—my name alone attracted thousands. I played for a while—to tell the truth, not the most difficult pieces, because I did not have time to practice—and then I got up from the piano and gave a speech about the fate of Poland, about the need to provide material aid to starving compatriots, and about the necessity of resurrecting an independent Poland.

Paderewski addresses a gathering of Polish organizations in America.

"Compatriots! Looking at your tired faces, at your hands thickened from hard work, looking at your modest attires—the rich and the proud, the happy and the envious may ask you about your rights to speak about your country. Answer them that you are the offspring of the Polish kings, that you are the heirs of the great Polish warriors, that you are sons of victorious Polish commanders, that you are children of Pułaski and Kosciuszko. Answer them hardily: that you are Poles!"

I was enflaming hearts. I was opening wallets. People became overwhelmed with enthusiasm. Polish emigrants in America felt themselves to be the depositories of the dream of the Independent. The Independent Poland.

On this enthusiasm I built a call for the creation of a Polish army in America. Volunteers began arriving in large numbers. Canada gave a military training base in Niagara-on-the-Lake, just below the famous waterfall. France sent blue uniforms and caps, but the Polish crowned eagles shone on them. England sent rifles.

I went to receive the parade of this army of mine, the Kosciuszko Army. Ah, how those boys marched. Mud was gushing under their boots. And I saw in them the Polish winged hussars.

He delivers a speech to the soldiers of Kosciuszko's Army on June 9, 1918, in Niagara-on-the-Lake:

"Officers and soldiers! Volunteers of our Polish Army! I come to you with a word of love on my lips, with immeasurable gratitude in my heart. I greet you with fraternal, joyful feelings and with the pride of a Pole. For I am proud that you are mine, and I am yours. For I am proud that in my veins your blood flows, that your tongue is mine, that you are our poor mother's Poland most beloved sons.

You are the soul of Polish emigration, the heart of all Poland. You carry in sacrifice to the Motherland all that you have the noblest—your zeal, courage and love; all that you have the most beautiful—your youth; all that you have the dearest—your life.

Go boldly. Go with faith in the sanctity of our cause, go with faith in victory! Go to battle, oh my Polish boys, my dearest, my beloved! May God makes you happy and bless you! Long live Poland! Our Polish Army long live!"

Ah, how these boys fought on the battlefields of France fighting the Germans. Many fell. For Poland. With the American corps that came to Europe, the Allies won the Great War. And the three powers which were enslaving Poland—yes, all three of them—lost the war, either beaten on the fronts or destroyed from within by revolutions.

Poland, thanks to this historic coincidence and thanks to God's miracle, was able to emerge independent. But it had to be rebuilt and strengthened. Its population must have been fed. The borders must have been demarcated and fortified. I undertook this effort.

I had the American government and the governments of the other Allies—Great Britain, France, Italy—behind me. I had the authorization of the Polish National Committee in Paris, which the Allies recognized as the provisional Polish government. I had the mandate of the American Polish community. I was enshrining the hopes of millions of my compatriots at home.

On an English warship I arrived in Gdańsk. From there—train to Poznań. At the very news that I had arrived the whole province rose up and threw off the German yoke.

From Poznań I went to Warsaw. At the train station I was greeted by a huge crowd. People unharnessed horses from the carriage prepared for me and with singing, with shouting, they dragged me all the way to the Bristol Hotel.

I stepped out onto the balcony. A sea of heads. A hundred thousand people.

I cast my eyes to the east—there's no border of the county. Only fires. I look to the west—thick, black clouds. But Poland is here. In the hearts of these people. Together we must extinguish fires, fence the land, strengthen it internally.

Paderewski speaks from the balcony of the Hotel Bristol.
"I did not come for eminence, fame, honor—but to serve. Yes, I came to serve, but not some single party. I respect all parties, but I do not belong to any. The party should be one: Poland. I will serve this one party until I die. The hour of resurrection has come. The resurrection of Poland. The joy of this moment must be transformed into the will to rebuild, to clean, and to put in order the homeland edifice so terribly destroyed by the foreigners. The enthusiasm must be transformed into the toil of daily work. Let us all get down to this work, as we are Poles. Long live the brightest, resurrected homeland, the mother of us all. Long live Poland!"

The crowds were overwhelmed with enthusiasm. I saw a sea of heads, and my gaze reached farther—to the millions of starved compatriots, to their ruined homes, and farther, towards the still uncertain and already burning borders of the Republic, our great Republic... I stood at her call.

Piłsudski ruled in Warsaw. He called himself the Commander, like Kosciuszko—but he was a dictator. He did not want me. He did not want to share power. However, he soon understood that if he did not put me at the head of the government, the Allies would not recognize Poland, would not send help, would not give loans. So Piłsudski appointed me the President of the Council of Ministers. I took the Ministry of Foreign Affairs as well. And to work. To the daily plowing, but with joy, because the plow puts down the slices of native, fertile soil. From it will raise a crop.

I formed the government. I appointed ministers. I organized elections to the Parliament. The Bristol Hotel soon proved too small to house the President and all the ministries. Therefore, I moved to the Warsaw Royal Castle.

The light illuminates the entire stage. We see a chamber—the office of Ignacy Paderewski at the Warsaw Castle. The desk; a telephone, papers, fountain pens; an armchair; a piano stool in front of the desk. Somewhere the map— which was already in use in the scene with President Wilson. Heaps of document. Paderewski looks around his office.

The Royal Castle. The office of the President of the Council of Ministers.

Paderewski sits down behind the desk.

Immediately a terrible clamor rang out. Does he want to become a king? So yelled the Parliament members, those great democrats, short-sighted screamers. So wrote the Masonic scribblers in the newspapers. So, supposedly, whispered the street.

In my soul, truly, Poland was still a kingdom. And me a king? I would carry the crown with dignity. But that was not what I aspired to. I aspired to give to the power of my office— legitimate Polish power, power finally Polish—a weight, splendor, and majesty. Yes, I constantly worked for Poland. Not for myself.

Mr. Secretary, please, announcing these gentlemen to me, give me their names, because I don't know them well yet. Who is the first to wait?

In the sequence that follows Paderewski addresses various people—he speaks to them and listens to them. At the same time, he occasionally takes a document from his desk, glances at it and signs it.

Mr. Wincenty Witos? Have a seat Mr. Chairman. I received from you and your People's Party a memorandum on the urgency of land reform. A reform? What kind of reform is that? It's simply—to grab the land form somebody and to give it to somebody else. Is it? I wholeheartedly stand with the Polish peasants, but this is not where we have to start to put Poland in order. First, we need to
strengthen those who feed the nation by farming their large estates, running true agricultural enterprises. That is, the landowners. We will return to the issue of reorganizing the ownership of Polish land. But first this land must be cultivated, sown, harvested. So, I put aside your memorandum and I'm asking you to encourage all peasants to work peacefully, and not to make claims. That's it, Mister Charmain.

The phone rings. Paderewski answers it.

Mr. Minister of Railways? He listens. I know this. The tracks to Lwów are blown up by the Ukrainians. You will contact Colonel Władysław Sikorski and under the protection of the army you will repair these tracks as soon as possible.

He greets another person.

Mr. Ignacy Daszynski? Leader of the Socialist Party? You are threatening me with a general strike if I do not agree to the inclusion of commissars elected by the workers to the managements of the factories. I will not agree to that. This smells of Bolshevism. This is not a civilized way to rebuild Polish industry. There will be no consent from me for this. First we must all, together, in unison, roll up our sleeves, rebuild factories, modernize them, intensify production. This is what you should preach at your rallies. Not calling for strikes. And if you ignite strikes, they will be broken by force. The audience is over.

He greets another person.

Member of Parliament Stanisław Grabski? Good morning, sir. Mr. Chairman Dmowski, my best, most loyal associate, respects you very much and recommends you to me. I thank you for the National Democratic Party's support for me in the Parliament, but I, dear sir, as I have already declared, and so I abide, I am not the President of the right-wing Government. I am the President of the Polish Government. Please, accept this declaration of mine and pass it on to all the deputies of your party.

This time he sees a group of people.

Esteemed professors? Welcome, dear sirs. I have invited you in such a large group and I hereby appoint you as members of the Governmental Codification Commission. I bestow on you a task to unify Polish law, then to codify it, and then to write the new Constitution of the Republic.

You say, Professor, that at the present time there are five legal orders left over from the times of foreign rule in Poland? Yes? Prussian law, Austrian law, Russian law, the law of the former Kingdom of Poland and, additionally, Hungarian law in the south provinces, yes? We need one law. Polish. Here is your task, honored gentlemen: to unify the law on the territory of the Republic. I give you one months to prepare a suitable bill, which the Government will introduce in the Parliament. And the Parliament will pass it. Then you will undertake work on the Constitution.

He greets another person.

Mr. Envoy Jałowiecki? Straight from the port of Gdańsk? I have read your reports. They still lie here. You organized well the reception of American aid, the unloading of ships, the sending food to the still starving country. As of today, I am elevating your rank. I appoint you Plenipotentiary Minister of the Government of the Republic for the Free City of Gdańsk. Be sure that the Polish flag flies high in Gdańsk.

Paderewski reaches for the telephone.

Mr. Minister of Post and Telegraph? I order, yes, Mr. Minister, yes, please treat this as an order, not as a recommendation, so, I order that by the end of February this year, yes, the end of February 1919, the stamps of the countries which previously ruled Poland be withdrawn from circulation and

Polish stamps be introduced. You will commission paintings for these stamps from the best painters. You will produce them. You will put them into circulation. I bid you farewell.

Mr. Secretary, many more visitors are waiting? I will receive all of them, even until the morning. But tomorrow I'm leaving for Paris for the Peace Conference. There will be a fight for Polish borders.

I went to this conference aware that by representing Poland, and being an internationally recognized artist, the cause of a resurrected Poland will rise to spiritual heights, and there will be a titanic struggle for its existence. And I will have to steadfastly defend universal values, the general good, and justice for all. And Polish interests. But I knew, at the same time, that on the level of politics, I will have to clash with the brutal, cynical, and ruthless struggle of all participants in this assembly for their own benefit.

He moves again to the center of the stage the map of Poland. He will mark on the map the territories that are being peeled away from the great Poland.

With this shape of great Poland, I lived. I had it in my memory and in my heart. But the mighty of this world, the so called Great Powers, caring only for their imperial interests, and not for the justice and rights of the Poles living in these lands, trimmed this Poland piece by piece.

The French did not want Poland to grow too strong, because they themselves and alone wanted to rule continental Europe. So, they truncated Poland from the west, did not give her wide access to the sea, made Gdańsk a free city, ordered plebiscites to be held in East Prussia and Silesia, and gave Russia, although newly communist, a huge chunk of our land in the east.

The British didn't want a big and strong Poland either. They wanted to continue doing business with Russia, whether white or red, and didn't mind that communism was already swelling there. So, they also trimmed us from the east.

The Americans, which were supposedly so magnanimous that they wanted to be good to all nations, decided to grant our south lands to the Czechs. Although President Wilson did not withdraw friendship from me, he had to reckon with other Allies, and as a result he sung the same tune as them.

I argued, proved, explained, persuaded. In vain. Poland existed, its very existence was defended, but our country was treated as a small pawn in the game between the superpowers. With a heavy heart I signed the peace treaty.

He removes the map.

When I returned to Warsaw, immediately the politicians jumped at me howling that I had not obtained enough.

Witos withdrew his People's Party support for me in the Parliament, screaming that I didn't care about the peasants, that I was – supposedly – going too much with the right. I wasn't going with any party, I was going with Poland.

Leader of the Socialists, Daszyński, accused me of overpaying the Americans for steam locomotives. These were the most modern, best machines in the world. They had to cost money and Poland needed them.

And I was no longer of any use to Piłsudski—the recognition of the Polish State on the international arena was obtained. I secured food from abroad, as well as supply of seed, machinery, clothing. Bankers gave me loans. I put the legal system in order. I implemented work on the unification of provinces separated for years by the foreigners.

Paderewski sees Józef Piłsudski entering his office.

Commander Piłsudski... I know how you, sir, are talking about me and what did you put into the heads of your supporters. That I came like a falcon released from the gauntlet of the American president to hunt for American business in the wilds of Eastern Europe. Or like a colonial corps general sent to Gdansk on an English warship to do British business here. Or that I wanted to bring French order to Poland with the help of my army waiting in France for my sign to enter the country and overthrow you. You disseminated such monstrosities about me. You mocked me that I am not a politician, but a third-rate pianist. Well, my rank as a pianist was somewhat better assessed by specialists. I was a pianist, yes, and in my music people all over the world heard for years our homeland's yearning for freedom and the will to regain that freedom.

And I was, above all, a man who selflessly serves the country purely out of love for it. A man who, like a simple fundraiser, collected money and food for hungry compatriots. I was supported by the entire American Polish community as well as all Poles scattered wherever bad fate threw them. The American government listened to me. I convinced all the Allies to the Polish cause. And the country? Poland awaited me as a Pole admired everywhere, as a generous philanthropist, and as a leader to whom the masses clung.

I did not oppose you! I wanted to bring you out of that socialist underground basement in which you had settled. I wanted to bring you into the great edifices of European politics. But you did not go with me. You envied me. For I was known all over the world, while you barely emerged from the mud of the trenches somewhere in the wilderness. And that I spoke a different language with each interlocutor. And even that I always dressed in dignity, while you took your stained gray uniform for a gala dress. And that you were a soldier, and I was an artist. You said that I cast a shadow over you. But I cooperated with you loyally. I asked your opinion many times. I showed courtesy. For which you treated me with a trashy, barracks language. I stood up for you in the Parliament when you were accused of thievery, of dictatorial inclinations—and rightly so.

I did not deny your merits. But it was not you alone who won Poland's independence. It was God who directed history and the course of the Great War so that the three oppressors of our country fell. Independence was won by the Nation itself, because in its very being it stored the outline of the edifice of the Independent. Only after that the independence was worked out by the emanations of the Nation—the great movements of the masses and their leaders. You were one of them. So was I.

For this independence's fortification I have harnessed myself as to the Herculean labor. Now the gusto must be turned into an iron. A conglomerate of aspirations and claims must be turned into a solid structure of a state ruled by law, in which everyone is equal. The state must be fortify it with institutions. But you want to govern yourself.

For now, you have the power—you have the power to rule alone. I am just an obstacle for you. I know that. I won't take up the dispute or fight with you because this would harm Poland. So, I resign of all my offices.

Paderewski stops addressing Piłsudski.
So, what is my balance sheet? A quarter-century of great worldwide success as a virtuoso and composer. Six years of political activity, including the leadership of the American Polish community, and then leading the government of Poland, as President of the Council of Ministers. I myself abandoned piano career for politics. I have now been shunned from politics by my compatriots at home. Is it necessary to venture out on a return journey? From politics back to music?

Pause.

Mr. Secretary! Everything has been packed as I ordered? My esteemed spouse was notified that the automobile departure to the Vienna Warsaw railway station is in an hour, right? To the people gathered in front of the Castle I will not speak. I will only greet them with a gesture.

Do not address me as "Mister President" anymore. My tenure is already over. Are you saying that this title will never depart from me? Thank you, Mister Secretary. And now I wish to be left alone.

He sits down behind his desk.
The desk of the former President.

He brings his big map. He spreads it out like a tablecloth on the desk.
Let this map stay here. So that my successor knows for sure that here one works for Poland. Only for Poland.

This time he does not speak to an imaginary figure but reaches into his memory.
Helena... We will return to the quiet and peaceful Switzerland. We will watch together from the bedroom window the pink dawns and orange sunsets of the snows of Mont Blanc.... Dark clouds obscuring the peaks of the Alps.... Mists pulling delicate curtains over the lake Geneva. No one and nothing shall separate us anymore. Not music, not politics, not people. Only death.

I remember when we were still young, yes, we used to be young, although today it's hard to believe... It was before we were married, you were still married.... not to me... I visited you in the evening... Your husband was not at home.... He was somewhere giving a concert on his singing violin.... I was afraid to be left alone with you.... I suggested we take a walk....

We stopped in the darkness on the banks of the river Seine...The lights of the gas lamps wavered on the water... Somewhere from behind us came the music of an accordion.... Paris... so the accordion.... something thoroughly banal.... and yet with an overwhelming power of mood.... It was early May.... the smell of chestnuts...

I longed to kiss you and put my arm around you gently, and you turned towards me, and I knew you wanted the same.... and more.... you wanted to return home with me.... dismiss the servants... But I, instead of kissing you, I said.... Helena, the time has come for us to stop the running away time.... And you looked at me radiantly, the whites of your eyes shone in the gloom like the two coins at the bottom of the Trevi fountain in Rome when we threw them in by the moon...

You said.... Yes, it's time... After all, we have been with each other forever, so we must remain until forever.... I did not understand your words, because we have not been together forever.... but I understood what you wanted to express through them.... This moment brought you out of time for me, only for me, and locked you back in time. Time before that moment was flowing, it was in motion, it was escaping, it was passing, it let itself be measured by days of longing, moments of seeing, and the time of that one moment stopped, no, it did not stop, rather it merged with eternity, so it became a time without time.... the time of my love for you....

Love? That love was indivisible, encompassing you, the music, and Poland. But then it began to diverge, to oppose each other.... Music and Poland were still one chord, but you introduced dissonances.... And then music and Poland went in two different directions, like a right hand and a left hand that don't catch the harmony.... For a pianist, it's a horror... Cold sweat... It's no longer "Tempo rubato", but a cacophony.... So, a desperate attempt to rebuild the polyphony.... It fails... It gets worse and worse... Fingers embrace frost.... Music... Poland... You... Which love?

You are no longer that woman from years ago. Poland has changed—from a dream of independence into an independence caricature. Music? It is the only one that is eternal. It lasts. One can descend into its abyss again.... Which, at the same time, is the road to the peaks.... Sinking into the depths—it is ascending to heaven. Will I be able to cope?

He changes his jacket for a tailcoat. The light dims. Only the sharp, narrow spotlight on Paderewski remains. He enters on the podium of a concert hall. There is a wild applause. Paderewski bows to the audience.
My first concert after a hiatus of so many years took place at the Carnegie Hall in New York, November 22, 1922. It gathered the *crème de la crème* of the music world. I was welcomed as a widely known and respected statesman—the entire audience rose reverently and applauded me for a long time. When I sat down at the piano there was an absolute silence. Now the pianist was to perform.

Paderewski sits down at the— imaginary—piano, just like at the beginning of the play. Only that now in the place where the piano would have been one can see—albeit indistinctly—the map of the Great Poland on the desk. Paderewski raises his hands— when he lowers them,
♪ Chopin's "Revolutionary Etude" erupts. Paderewski plays for a moment, then turns to the audience and speaks while the piano continues to sound:
Scream! That terrible scream of pain and hurt. Even more desperate than before, because now Chopin's pain is multiplied by my pain.

♪ The music continues.

Paderewski speaks to the audience.
The left hand, with horror, sweeps some debris, ruins, runs back and forth across some barely cold battlefields, again, and again, and again. The right hand wants to fight, but it collapses under the onslaught of waves of lamentations, assaults of suffering, strokes of pain—which every now and then fall on it from a sky-high height, pushing it to the very bottom of the dark abyss.

Both hands make a brief attempt to silence the scream, to forget. In vain! The left hand is unable to stop its run through the dark labyrinths. And the right hand screams again tearfully, no longer singing, no longer touching the keys, but pounding on the bare strings, struggling, as if it wanted to smash, shatter the keyboard, the whole piano, break out the iron bars that snap on all sides.

The fight is on. A storm of sounds is raging. The right hand seems to be catching up with the left hand, it leaves it alone for a moment in its terrific rush, it levels a breathless run with it. There is no agreement. There is defiance. There is no consolation. There is protest. There is no solace. There is despair. So, the melody descends into the melt of hopelessness, embraced by darkness.

Only for a moment does hope for the victory of light over darkness dawns, like a ray of sunshine suddenly ejaculating from among the storm clouds, but it is only for a moment. The pain consumes it again.

♪ *The music ends. Frantic applause erupts. Against its backdrop, Paderewski speaks:*

Return?

This concert of mine was described as one of the greatest events in the history of music of the first quarter of the 20th century. There were speculations that it would remain the greatest, most important event in the history of music of the entire century. In the history of music in general? It was written and said that I played again with absolute perfection. Listeners, the music world, fellow artists, critics, impresarios were enchanted, delighted, enthralled. After this concert I began to be called "immortal".... I had to encore countless times.

Among other pieces, I always played for an encore my favorite *Minuet A l'Antique*. Serenity—reverie—mystery...

He sits down at the piano.

♪ *He plays "Minuet A l'Antique".*

And again, after a few bars he begins to speak while the music continues.

...It is like someone trying to smooth the floor with a light foot.... One and two... one and two... Already in the first bars I introduce the basic theme – simple, graceful, melodious.... Then, there is a growing opposition between gentleness, restraint and modesty, and the temptation to sing loudly, dance fast, burst with joy. Oh, yes, oh, yes, oh, yes, I let myself run wildly across the keyboard, and my fingers make strokes as swift and skillful as only I can...

Now, I seem to be musing, as if listening to myself, as if recalling phrases of a Chopin mazurka I once heard. Oh, I always bowed my head to Chopin, I attentively listened to his music...

Echoes of Chopin awake the echoes of the Polish landscape in early autumn, here and there, punctuated by the rays of the setting sun, wrapped in a mysterious Polish sadness.

The rural landscape seems to expand, encompassing a ballroom in some palace, where the shadows of dancing couples swirl. The singing transforms into whispering, in which there are some vague questions, repeated and processed, and never finding an answer. A mysterious ritual of beauty continues, towards which one can look, but only for a moment, as through a half-opened door....

Mad applause.
I'm back.
I returned to the piano. I returned to the concert halls.

Actor performing Paderewski bows to the audience. There is— hopefully— an applause of the spectators.

Actor acknowledges the applause. Then takes off his tailcoat and addresses the spectators:

Dear all, with Maestro Paderewski we have returned to the kingdom of music. He reigned in it again. And he reigned in it for the next long years.

For many Poles Paderewski remained a source of encouragement and hope, a model of integrity and patriotism, as well as personal diligence and selfless service to the country. He focused the love of millions of Poles. For years he was the best known and most respected Pole in the world. His concerts continued to attract thousands of enthusiastic listeners.

But once more he was driven away from the piano by the war. For in 1939, Poland was once again attacked and invaded by two evil neighbors—Hitler's German Reich and Stalin's Soviet Union. They divided Poland between the two of them. So, Paderewski again took up the task of working for Poland. With this mission he went, as he had done years before, to America. Here, his heart could not withstand the hardships of travels, speeches, conferences, meetings, interviews.... He died in 1941. By the executive decision of President Roosevelt, he was buried with the honors due to the head of state in Arlington Military Cemetery.

When Poland again broke out into independence Paderewski's ashes were brought to Warsaw in 1992. He was back!

♪ *Bells rang out—from numerous churches—far and near.*

Actor descends from the stage and—followed by a spotlight—merges with the spectators.

He is back! Ah, I can see him! He is there! High up! Again, he appears on the balcony of the Bristol Hotel. Again—before him a sea of heads. He is there! He is there on the balcony. And I am in that crowd. I call out to him: Maestro Paderewski, return Poland to us! Save Poland again! Save Poland!

Standing there, on that balcony today, Paderewski has the knowledge of the terrible fate of Poland, first occupied by enemies during World War II, and then betrayed by the Allies, as once at the Paris Peace Conference, the same years later at the Yalta Conference. He watched in despair at the subsequent truncation of Poland's eastern territories—again a red line wounding his great map. He saw how hard was the fate of Poles in the shackles of communism. He rejoiced when the Poles, inspired by the Polish Pope, ignited the great Solidarity movement and regained their freedom.

And now they are again losing their freedom, their sovereignty, their identity—coerced by foreign dictates, overpowered by their own stupidity.

Paderewski casts his gaze eastward—Poland's borders again in danger.

Paderewski looks west—morally corrupted Europe, America collapsing into tyranny, all over the globe the madness of globalism.

Maestro Paderewski—Save Poland! Speak the word! Speak the word!

♪ *The bells are still ringing. Actor silences them with gestures of both hands— like a conductor of an orchestra.*

If he spoke, he would have one message for us: Poland! Stand by Poland! Stand by your country!

If he played the piano, there would be Poland in it—as the poet says—Poland at the zenith of its perfection.

Actor returns on the stage. He puts on a tailcoat.

This is what Maestro Paderewski left us as his political testament: Poland! Stand by Poland!

This is what Maestro Paderewski left us as an artistic testament: Soar with art into the world of the spirit!

With this we part.

Actor bows to the audience. The audience's applause—hopefully—erupts. Actor bows again and is about to leave the stage. He stops. He returns hastily. He silences the audience with a gesture.

I forgot one more thing. Ignacy Paderewski still left us something.

Actor pulls out from under the desk a box containing a bottle (or more bottles) of "Paderewski Zinfandel" wine and a basket of glasses. There is also a knife and a corkscrew. Actor cuts off the silverware surrounding the cork and opens the bottle with the corkscrew. He speaks during these activities:

Ladies and gentlemen, Ignacy Paderewski, in addition to his political testament and in addition to his artistic testament, also left us this excellent "Paderewski Zinfandel" wine. Perhaps someone would like to help me... This bottle... Glasses... Please help... Let's set the glasses here... Please pour....

Actor invites someone from the audience to help uncork the bottle, another person to set the glasses at the edge of the stage, and another to pour wine into glasses. He speaks during these activities.

Ignacy Paderewski once purchased two ranches in California. He named them "San Ignacio" and "Santa Helena"—his, and his wife's, names. He made wine there—until he decided to return to piano. "Paderewski Zinfandel" is a variety of the Zinfandel strain, but a special one, just his, Paderewski's—"Paderewski Zinfandel".

Actor walks off the stage and encourages the audience to reach for the glasses, clinking glasses with them. A situation like a social party is created. Actor continues:

Let's try it... The bouquet... Special light color...But it's not a white wine.... Although it is not a rosé either. It has an amber color, as if with a touch of California sequoia bark.... Or rather, gold, dark California gold.... To the traditional astringency of white wine, it just adds that disturbing, slightly bitter, taste. To the Master's health!

Actor mingles with the audience. He strikes up conversations with spectators. He walks among them distributing glasses. He clicks his glass with theirs. He exchanges remarks. He raises—together with the audience members—toasts in honor of Ignacy Paderewski.

THE END

Buffalo – Los Angeles, 2022

≡ ∫∫∫ ≡

LIST OF MUSICAL PIECES INTRODUCED IN THE ACTION

Fryderyk Chopin:
    Revolutionary Etude, Opus 10, No. 12
    (1) the whole piece
    (2) just the beginning
    (3) the whole piece

Ignacy Paderewski:
    Piano Concerto in A minor, Opus 17 – the beginning
    Polish Fantasy in G-sharp Minor, Opus 19 – the beginning
    Symphony in B-minor, Polonia
    Humoresque, opus 14 – the whole piece
    Minuet A l'Antique in G major, Opus 14/1 – the whole piece

PADEREWSKI'S CHILDREN

A PLAY IN TWO PARTS

CAST
PART 1
Colonel LePan
Lieutenant John Chwalski
Second Lieutenant Zgmunt Dygat, pianist
Sergeant Cox
Mary
Soldiers of The Kościuszko Army
Soldier 1
Soldier 2
Soldier 3
Soldier 4
Soldier 5
Soldier 6
Girls–Members of Vocal & Leonce Ensemble of the Buffalo's Mickiewicz Society
Mary
Girl 1
Girl 2
Girl 3
PART 2
Professor Zygmunt Dygat (previously Sec. Lieut. Dygat)
Colonel John Chwalski (previously Lieut. Chwalski)
Zofia, Professor Dygat's wife

Members of The Clandestine Theater

Mieczysław, director
Danuta, actress
Hala, actress
Barbara, actress
Leon, pianist
Bogdan, actor
Hala's son, five years old
Germans
Plain cloth agent
Gestapo man
Gestapo man

PLACES AND TIMES

Part 1. The military camp at Niagara-on-the-Lake, Ontario, Canada in 1918.

Part 2. A home at the suburb of Cracow, Poland, Summer and Fall of 1941

NOTES

The character of Ignacy Paderewski is presented as a marionette. The marionette is about 35 inch tall.

Live piano music performed in the play is its indispensable element. Because of this the character of the Second Lieutenant Zgmunt Dygat (later Professor Dygat) should be performed by and actor-pianist.

≡ ∫∫∫ ≡

PROLOGUE

A projection of of the beginning of the film "The Moonlight Sonata" (about three minutes) in which we see Ignacy Paderewski giving a piano concert.

The military camp of the Polish Kosciuszko Army at Niagara-on-the-Lake, Ontario, Spring 1918.

A large entrance gate with an inscription on top "The Polish Kosciuszko Army Camp. Niagara-on-the-Lake. 1918. Za wolność naszą i waszą."

A fragment of an assembly ground in the camp.

A military canteen with a small stage and a piano.

The office of Colonel LePan, the commander of the camp: a Colonel's desk, Sergeant Cox desk, a stand with three flags Polish, Canadian, American

SCENE 1

♪ *Military band is playing a march off stage.*

The projection of the Niagara Falls view form the Canadian side.

The Colonel is talking on the phone. Sergeant Cox is busy with paperwork. On the assembly ground Soldiers go through morning drill.

COLONEL: Yes, yes, yes... You've already told me that six times. Yes, general. I do keep a log of my phone calls. You've promised me six times to ship an additional 4 000 rifles and 280 000 rounds of munitions. What's more, you've promised me... how many times.. yes... I got it... you've promised me nine times to ship 22 000 gas masks, yes, 22 000. Yes, general, I understand the war situation, I understand that the Americans equip their own troops first, but we have a signed agreement, president Wilson is personally looking after this Polish Army, and I can't accept any more delays. These boys must be properly equipped and trained before I send them into the trenches in Europe. I want...

Lieutenant Chwalski enters, salutes, and waits at the door. The Colonel keeps talking. The military band gradually fades out.

I won't let them be caught in a round of German gas without these masks. I simply refuse to ship them over to France. Yes, general, you can call it insubordination! You can court-martial me! I will take full responsibility. I am expecting you to phone me back within a few hours with a clear statement as to when I'm going to get these masks. What? The troopships are scheduled to sail from Montreal in four weeks? You're telling me to be ready? I'm telling you to allow me to be ready! I will not be ready without rifles and, especially, not without gas masks. If I am not going to get them by next week, I will call Maestro Paderewski and he'll certainly call President Wilson. And the President will ask you what happened. You. Not me. Good bye, sir.

He puts aside the telephone.

Lieutenant Chwalski?

LIEUTENANT: Yes, sir. Lieutenant Chwalski, as ordered, sir.

COLONEL: Let's hear your report.

LIEUTENANT: Sir, you ordered me to prepare the master plan for Maestro Paderewski's visit for the review of the troops just before they embark for Europe, sir.

COLONEL: There'll be no visit unless we get these gas masks.

LIEUTENANT: Sir? *Pause.* Should I scrap the plans then?

COLONEL: No. But don't be surprised if they're scrapped at the last minute.

LIEUTENANT: Yes, sir. Do you want to hear what I propose, in case Maestro's visit goes on as scheduled.

COLONEL: Report. Quickly. I have several calls to make.

LIEUTENANT: Yes, sir. Maestro Paderewski and his party will travel by automobiles from Buffalo, arriving before noon. I propose, A, to put up an arch of honor at the entrance to the camp with a suitable inscription; B, to have all men in full battle dress and gear...

COLONEL: We're lacking four thousand rifles. Not to mention gas masks. Continue, please.

LIEUTENANT: ...all men in formation on the Parade ground. At the very moment Maestro's car stops, they'll shout "Hurrah!" and "Niech żyje," that's in Polish, and they'll continue shouting until the Maestro gets out of the car and is greeted by you, sir.

COLONEL: Very good. Go on.

LIEUTENANT: Then the troops will be dismissed and you'll invite the Maestro and his party to lunch in the officers' canteen.

COLONEL: All right. Go on.

LIEUTENANT: After lunch the Maestro will attend the military parade of the troops. The marching band will play. Maestro might make a speech.

COLONEL: A parade? The There's not enough arms. I told you. Go on.

LIEUTENANT: In the afternoon, you, sir, you propose to the Maestro and his party's a visit to Niagara Falls and you accompany him.

COLONEL: All right. Go on.

LIEUTENANT: You'll return and there will be a regimental dinner with the Maestro, Madame Paderewska, other officials, the press, and you, sir, presiding. You, sir, will make a toast and Maestro Paderewski, I presume, will make a speech.

COLONEL: All right. Accepted. Thank you, lieutenant.

LIEUTENANT: Sir, you're welcome, sir. But that's not all, sir.

The soldiers have finished the morning drill.

COLONEL: After dinner all are dismissed. The troops to the barracks. The guests to the hotel. Thank you, lieutenant.

LIEUTENANT: Sir, you're welcome, sir. But there's one more point of the program after dinner.

COLONEL: What's that? Rapport.

LIEUTENANT: Sir, I propose to prepare a theater production in honor of the Maestro, sir.

COLONEL: Theater? We don't have such nonsense here.

LIEUTENANT: Sir, if you'll allow me to explain, sir?

COLONEL: Theater? Do you have a stage? Do you have a play? Do you have actors?

LIEUTENANT Sir...

COLONEL: All right. Go ahead. But I'm busy.

LIEUTENANT: Sir, a theater can be put together in the canteen. As far as the play is concerned, I'm a poet, I never mentioned that because it did not matter from a military point of view, but, yes, I'm a poet, and, actually, I have written a play about Maestro's life and works. Some of the boys would make fine actors, and, to tell the truth, I have already enquired about the women. Because we would need women too. They are available, sir.

COLONEL: Available? Women? In this camp? I'll never allow that! It's a barracks, not a brothel.

LIEUTENANT: But, sir, I'm not talking about... women... you know... such women... I'm talking about actresses and dancers. As I said, I made an inquiry. There's a theater and dance company in Buffalo. Just across the border. They are called "The Mickiewicz Society."

COLONEL: Mickiewicz? (*He mispronounces.*) I never heard about her.

LIEUTENANT: Him, sir. He was a poet. Poland's greatest poet. A man, sir. Mickiewicz.

COLONEL: Mickiewicz? So, what about this Mickiewicz, poet? Does he live in Buffalo? Why not have him write a play for us, since he is the greatest Polish poet?

LIEUTENANT: Sir, it's impossible, sir. He's dead.

COLONEL: Dead? What happened?

LIEUTENANT: He died on cholera in France years ago.

COLONEL: In France? That's where many of our boys will die... We must get this armament. Proper training will diminish our losses...

LIEUTENANT: Yes, sir. To get back to my project. The girls from

"The Mickiewicz Society" can act in my play, but only, of course, if you, sir, agree and give me authorization to go ahead with the project.

♪ *The telephone rings. The Colonel picks it up.*

COLONEL: Colonel LePan. *He listens.* Yes, sir. I will be ready, sir. I thank you, general.

He puts down the phone.

The rifles are coming from the Buffalo Armory tomorrow, by the direct order of president Wilson. I like that. The gas masks will be delivered in three days. I like that even more. Maestro Paderewski offered to pay for them out of his own pocket. His visit is on. He'll arrive this Saturday. You have five days to prepare everything.

LIEUTENANT: Yes, sir. But what about my theater project?

COLONEL: Do whatever you want, lieutenant. I put you in charge. But if you don't make the Maestro happy, you'll find out how miserable life in a penal squad can be.

LIEUTENANT: Yes, sir. I'll not disappoint you, sir. May I submit the play for your approval, sir?

COLONEL: No. I don't have time. You're responsible. As I said.

♪ *Telephone rings.*

COLONEL: Dismissed.

Lieutenant Chwalski salutes and exits. Colonel LePan picks up the phone.

COLONEL: The poet in uniform... No! No poet here. It's Colonel LePan. I'm listening. I can't take any more volunteers, general. No. We are already overcrowded. We're lacking beds, arms, everything. Open another camp, general, for these newcomers. Now, when America finally gets into the war you can establish it on your territory. In Lewiston, across the river, or somewhere. *He listens for a long time.* Yes, sir. If there's is an agreement between Britain, Canada, the United States, and Poland... Yes, sir. I'll open a new sub-camp for them. But you furnish the uniforms, those blue French ones, the arms, and don't forget about the gas masks. I'll cable you the numbers once I've seen these new recruits, given them the medical, and made my selection. I can turn them into soldiers in three months. Those who make it through the training will be ready by September. Yes, this year, 1918. *He throws the telephone.* Not enough money in Washington, but they keep sending me men.

Sergeant approaches the Colonel.

COLONEL: What's that, sergeant?

SERGEANT: Sir, this lieutenant Chwalski fellow, the poet, he's going to bring disgrace and disorder to the camp, sir.

COLONEL: How?

SERGEANT: These boys must train hard and deep in the Canadian mud here if they are to survive over there, in the French mud and trenches, sir. Not to make stage plays. Chwalski may keep soldiers from drill and training. And he wants to bring women into the camp? It's just not done, sir. There are special military brothels for this. There'll be trouble, sir.

COLONEL: You shall see to it that the drill, rout marches, and morale are not compromised by the theater.

SERGEANT: Is that an order, sir?

♪ *The telephone rings. Colonel picks it up.*

COLONEL: What? An accident in training? Amputation? All right, doctor, I'm on my way to the hospital. Poor boy. He'll not see France. Word of comfort needed.

He exits, followed by the sergeant.

♪ *The Military band plays a march.*

SCENE 2

Five days later. Soldiers in dirty training uniforms with rifles, backpacks, and gas masks hurry in the canteen. They put aside their gear and get to work, preparing the canteen for the rehearsal. They stand at attention in a line in front of the stage as lieutenant Chwalski enters. The lieutenant carries a marionette of Ignacy Paderewski.

LIEUTENANT: At ease! Is everything ready for the rehearsal?

SOLDIERS: Yes, sir!

SOLDIER 1: Sir, may I ask a question, sir?

LIEUTENANT: Speak.

SOLDIER 1: Sir, we are preparing a show. But Sergeant Cox says he's not going to allow it. He says this is a military camp, not a brothel.

LIEUTENANT: Sergeant Cox, like everybody else, must obey orders. And we have been ordered by the colonel to get the show ready. Maestro Paderewski's coming tomorrow. This is our last rehearsal. Do you know your lines?

SOLDIER 1: I do, sir.

LIEUTENANT: And the rest of you?

ALL SOLDIERS: Yes, sir.

SOLDIER 2: Sir, I have a proposal, sir. I play Maestro's Paderewski's music teacher in Warsaw. I feel awkward saying "You, dumb head, you'll never be a pianist." I would rather say, "You, honorable Maestro, you'll never be a pianist." This will sound more polite. Or, even better, "You, honorable Maestro, you'll make a fine career as a pianist."

LIEUTENANT: But the point is that the Maestro was not yet a Maestro at that time and nobody believed that he was going to make a fine career. Do you understand?

SOLDIER 2: No. The Maestro is a Maestro. I don't want to offend him.

LIEUTENANT: Simply shut up, and say what you've been told to say.

SOLDIER 2: Yes, sir. "You dumb head Maestro, you'll never be a pianist."

LIEUTENANT: Shut up. Not now. And cut "Maestro." Only "dumb head." Got it?

SOLDIER 2: Yes, sir. "You dumb head," sir.

All soldiers laugh.

SOLDIER 3: Sir, is it true that Maestro Paderewski is a real millionaire, sir?

LIEUTENANT: Why?

SOLDIER 3: Because if he was a real millionaire, why would he care about buying us gas masks?

LIEUTENANT: He can pay for our gas masks precisely because he is a millionaire. He bought them for our safety and for the good of our country.

SOLDIER 3: What country, sir?

LIEUTENANT: Poland, of course.

SOLDIER 3: Not America, sir?

LIEUTENANT: America too. America and Poland are allies. Got it?

SOLDIER 3: I don't get it. Real millionaires don't give their money away for any country. They keep it for themselves.

LIEUTENANT: No. These are the false millionaires. The misers. The real ones are generous. They support their countries. Enough of these stupid questions.

SOLDIER 1: Sir?

LIEUTENANT: Yes?

SOLDIER 1: Sir, what do you have, there, under your arm, sir? Is this the puppet of Maestro Paderewski?

LIEUTENANT: It's not a puppet. It's a marionette.

SOLDIER 1: Of the Maestro? Does he have such red hair? Like a red fox. *All laugh.*

LIEUTENANT: Be quiet. The Maestro doesn't have red hair. He has golden hair.

SOLDIER 2: But that one has carrot red. The troops will love it. *All laugh.*

LIEUTENANT: Quiet. Silence.

SOLDIER 4: Sir, one more question, sir, please?

LIEUTENANT: What is it, now?

SOLDIER 4: Is it true that Madame Paderewski has a chicken farm in Switzerland? And she sends the Maestro to feel hens for eggs? *He suddenly bursts into a chicken imitating sound*: Co... coo... co... co... coo... *All Soldiers laugh.*

LIEUTENANT: Attention. This yank mockery of Maestro Paderewski will cease! You should be proud to have the honor of performing for Maestro and his honorable wife...

Second Lieutenant Dygat enters.

LIEUTENANT DYGAT: I'm not late, am I?

LIEUTENANT: You are, indeed. You were supposed to bring the girls in from the check point. Where are they?

LIEUTENANT DYGAT: The guards didn't want to let them in. But here they are, waiting...

Lieutenant Chwalski goes to the entrance and calls.

LIEUTENANT: Ladies... Sorry... Girls... I'm sorry... Actresses... Dancers... Singers... Whatever... This way, please.

A group of young girls in traditional Polish folk costumes ("stroje krakowskie") enter. They are shy and keep close together. They curtsy and run to a corner of the space.

LIEUTENANT: Thank you for coming... Well... Are we all ready?

The women look at each other and suddenly burst into song and dance of "The Last Mazur."

LIEUTENANT, *gently interrupts them after a few bars*: It's nice that you prepared that song and dance, but we have to proceed in the proper order. It comes later in the show. Everybody! Places, please!

The girls take their positions in the wings. The Soldiers stay motionless at attention.

LIEUTENANT: What happened? Go! What's wrong with you?

SOLDIER 1: Sir...

LIEUTENANT: Yes?

SOLDIER: You didn't order the troops "At ease." We are still on "Attention."

LIEUTENANT: All right, all right... At ease, then. Places.

Four soldiers run onto the stage and disappear behind the curtain. Two others—assigned to technical tasks—go to the curtain and the light board.

LIEUTENANT: Zygmunt, to the piano!

Lieutenant Dygat sits at the piano and immediately starts playing a Polka.

LIEUTENANT: Not the Polka! Not now! Not the Polka! Stop it! Get ready to play the introductory piece first, and, then the "March of the Falcons." But wait for the cue. You know it?

LIEUTENANT DYGAT: Sure...

LIEUTENANT, *loud*: Everyone, we are going to start the rehearsal. It's our last rehearsal, so be focused and do precisely what you were told. Music! Lights! Curtain!

♪ *Lieutenant Dygat plays a military march. The lights focus on the curtain. The curtain opens. The Soldiers march onto the stage, stop, and stand at "Attention" on one side of the stage. The women enter marching, stop, and stand still at the other side. Lieutenant Chwalski appears in the center. After a while he starts shouting*

LIEUTENANT: Stop, stop playing. Stop.

Music stops. When you see me here you have to stop playing. I'll have a speech now. Got it?

LIEUTENANT DYGAT: Sure...

LIEUTENANT: Honorable Maestro! Madame Helena Paderewska! Colonel LePan! Distinguished guests! Ladies and gentlemen! Soldiers! We are happy to be visited by our most beloved leader and father, Maestro Ignacy Paderewski, creator of this Polish Army, which is going to fight Poland's enemies and liberate our motherland from the oppression of Prussia, Austria, and Russia. Welcome Maestro! *He poses and looks at Lieutenant Dygat who—in turn—looks at him, smiling.*

After a while, Lieutenant Chwalski shouts: Dygat! "The Falcons!" Remember! Play now!

♪ *Dygat plays the "March of the Falcons" and all on stage sing.*

Music and song end. Lieutenant continues:

In honor of our honorable Maestro, his honorable wife, and his honorable staff and guests, as well as for the enlightenment of the troops, we have prepared a modest production presenting the life of the Maestro. But an insurmountable obstacle appeared. Nobody dared to impersonate the Maestro. Indeed, the greatest actors would tremble at the very thought of playing a character of such magnitude. We are only simple amateurs. What to do? Out of necessity we decided to use a marionette to represent the Maestro. A marionette is an ancient, noble, and artistic device. We hope that you, Maestro, will accept and bless our efforts.

After a pause, he shouts: Curtain! "Our efforts" was the cue for closing the curtain. *The curtain closes and Lieutenant steps in front of it.* Here we go… Dygat! Music! Mazurka!

Lieutwennant Dygat plays the nostalgic Chopin's Mazurka in A minor Op. 59, No 1, while Lieutenant Chwalski starts the narration.

NOTE: The following scene is a clumsy amateur theatre. The performers—the soldiers and the girls. use exaggerated gestures and speech. Lieutenant Chwalski delivers the narration and operates the marionette of Paderewski.

LIEUTENANT: Maestro Ignacy Paderewski was born in 1860, in Eastern Poland—which was at that time under Russian rule—to an ancient, noble, yet impoverished, family.

Curtain opens and we see a crib rocked by Mother (performed by Woman 3). A Father (played by Soldier 4) stands on the other side of the crib. Two Soldiers hold a sign Kurylovka Estate, Poland, 1860.

LIEUTENANT: Alas, the Maestro's mother died soon after giving birth, and his father was arrested for supporting the Polish uprising against the Russians.

The woman on stage falls to the floor. Two Russian soldiers (Performed by Soldier 1 and Soldier 3) put chains on Father's hands and take him away. Curtain closes and music stops.

LIEUTENANT *continues*: Upon his release from prison the Maestro's father educated him at home and hired a piano teacher for him. Seeing the musical talent of his son, he sent him to the Music Institute in Warsaw.

Curtain opens. A small piano (a toy size) sits in the center. Two Soldiers hold a sign Warsaw 1872. *Lieutenant Chwalski introduces the marionette of Paderewski on the stage and sits it at the piano. The marionette "plays" piano making awkward and funny movements.*

♪ *Lieutenant Dygat plays Bach's Italian Concerto—he hits the keys too hard and stumbles every other bar. Piano Teacher (performed by Soldier 2) appears and listens.*

PIANO TEACHER, *interrupting Paderewski*: No, no, no! Your playing is horrible. You, honorable Maestro, you'll never be a pianist. That is, you, dumb head redhead, you'll never be a pianist. Sorry, Lieutenant, I couldn't help...

LIEUTENANT: I told you! And there's no "redhead", only "dumb head." Take it again and continue.

PIANO TEACHER: No, no, no! Your playing is horrible. You, dumb head, you'll never be a pianist. You'd better play a trombone or a horn. Never the piano. Never.

Paderewski's (marionette) knocks his head on the piano—Lieutenant Dygat hits several keys at once. The curtain is drawn. Lieutenant Chwalski appears in front of the curtain.

LIEUTENANT: Young Paderewski was terribly ashamed and disappointed, yet the professor's remarks did not crush him. On the contrary, he worked even harder than before. He mobilized his will power, his famous will power which would eventually lead him to stardom. He soon graduated from the Warsaw Music Institute *Magna Cum Laude*, was employed as a professor of piano there, and started to give public concerts, to critical acclaim.

♪ *Curtain opens. Two Soldiers hold a sign* Warsaw, 1878. *Young Paderewski (marionette) plays Chopin's Scherzo No.1 in B-minor, Op. 20.(The marionette is operated by Lieutenant Chwalski and Lieutenant Dygat plays piano.) Only a few bars of the opening are played. Curtain closes.*

LIEUTENANT: Paderewski himself knew that he was playing well, but he also knew that he had to learn more to improve his technique. Yet he was poor and had no money to study abroad. Providential assistance came from Helena Modjeska, a famous actress, who, after a brilliant career on the Polish stages, had emigrated to America and become a star there. During one of her visits to the mother-country she heard Paderewski play. She was enchanted.

♪ *Curtain opens. Two soldiers hold a sign* Cracow, 1884. *Young Paderewski (marionette) plays Chopin's Scherzo No. 2 in B-flat minor, Op. 31. (Again, the marionette is operated by Lieutenant Chwalski; Lieutenant Dygat plays piano.) Helena Modjeska (performed by Mary) stands at the piano and listens.*

HELENA MODJESKA: Ignacy, you have a talent like fire. You must develop it into conflagration. You're skills are great, but they must be perfected. Here's what we'll do. We'll give a joint concert. I'll play scenes from my most famous roles and you'll play Chopin and Liszt. The public will come to see Modjeska, of course, and they'll pay generously for the tickets. With the money from the show—I'll add something to it—you'll go to Vienna for master classes with the finest European pedagogue, Theodore Leszetycki. You'll conquer Vienna. Then you'll go to Paris, London, and then, I hope, you'll come to my America. I see for you a great career. I believe in you. Have courage and work hard!

Curtain closes. Lieutenant Chwalski appears.

LIEUTENANT: So Modjeska raised money for Paderewski's studies in Vienna. But once again, he had to learn the hard way...

♪ *Curtain opens. Two Soldiers hold a sign* Vienna, 1885. *Young Paderewski (marionette) is again at the piano playing Beethoven's Sonata in B-flat, Op. 27. Professor Leszetycki (played by Soldier 1) enters and listens. Again, Lieutenant Chwalski operates the marionette and Lieutenant Dygat plays piano.*

PROFESSOR LESZETYCKI: *Interrupting Paderewski* You have a certain technique, Mr. Paderewski, but you make horrible mistakes. Your hands were not trained properly by your previous teachers. You're already twenty-five. You're too old to start building your technique from scratch. You'll never be a real pianist, no! I don't have time for you. Good bye.

Curtain draws. Lieutenant Chwalski appears.

LIEUTENANT: What a terrible blow! Once again, the future Maestro mobilized his entire will power. He convinced professor Leszetycki to give him lessons. He practiced day and night for twelve, or even seventeen hours without rest. After two years of intense training he made his international debut in Vienna. He received enthusiastic applause from the public and acclaimed reviews from the critics. But this was only his first step. Paris was the music capital of the world at that time.

♪ *Curtain opens. Two Soldiers hold a sign* Paris, 1888. *Paderewski is again at the piano and plays Chopin's from No. 16 in B-flat minor of the "24 Preludes" Op. 28. Again, Lieutenant Chwalski operates the marionette and Lieutenant Dygat plays piano. Paderewski finishes. All Men and Women appear on stage applauding loudly. A newspaper boy (played by Soldier 4) runs in front of the stage and distributes newspapers to the men and women. They read them, shouting from the stage to the public, while Lieutenant Dygat accentuates each statement with a strong chord on the piano.*

- "Paris, March 4, 1888. Yesterday's concert in Salle Erard by Ignacy Paderewski was an all out victory for the young Polish pianist. The public was carried away... "

- "The esoteric essence of music transpires through his hands. Like Shakespeare's Prospero he rules spirits and nature."

- "The notes drop from his fingers as tears of the mythical Niobe, or fall as blood's drops of the fighting Olympic heroes. His music brings to mind endless Odysseus's journeys on the stormy waves, or on the calm harbor of Ithaca."

- "His music climbs the highest peaks of heaven and provokes thunder. Then, he envelops the enchanted listeners with a sky full of clouds, now light, now stormy."

- "Paderewski's mastery, his wonderful touch, a completely fresh combination of intellectualism with sensualism, a song drawn from the piano, and the incredible power of his strokes overwhelm the listeners."

- "He is a poet of the piano, and he plays piano as he would play all the instruments of a symphonic orchestra at once."

- "Paderewski is a genius who, in addition, plays piano."

Curtain closes.

LIEUTENANT: After Paris, London fell to its knees. Queen Victoria invited the young virtuoso to play for her in her private apartments in Windsor. Society ladies, artists, gentlemen, and politicians wanted to meet him. The famous painters begged him to model for them. But there was another step to take on the way to the stars. America.

♪ *Curtain opens. Two Soldiers hold a sign* New York, 1891. *Paderewski (the marionette) at the piano. Lieutenant Dygat plays Chopin's Etude No.12 in C-minor, Op. 10. Soldiers and Girls applaud. Mr. Steinway (played by Soldier 3) appears at the piano.*

MR. STEINWAY: My name is Steinway. Yes. It's me, in person. The owner and head of the famous Steinway piano manufacturing company. My dear Paderewski, you came, you played, you conquered. America is at your feet. What's more, there's a lot of money at your feet. I propose a tour of 109 concerts over 130 days, one thousand dollars per concert. Not bad, eh? You'll be playing on my pianos exclusively. The Steinway marquee and your endorsement—"Steinway is the best piano in the world"—will appear on every poster and program, and you'll mention Steinway, the name of my company, in every interview. Deal?

Curtain closes.

LIEUTENANT: Paderewski's first tour of America made him a star, the second, two years later, a legend. But it was still an uphill struggle. During this second tour, practicing, as usual for hours day and night, Paderewski injured his finger. The fourth finger of his right hand. The doctors' treatment did not help. The next sold out concert was approaching rapidly.

♪ *Curtain opens. Two Soldiers hold a sign* Boston, 1893. *Paderewski (the marionette) at the piano, his right hand covered by white scarf. Dygat shows how Paderewski tries to play the same piece as before, but makes errors. Doctor (performed by Soldier 4) appears.*

DOCTOR: I categorically forbid you to play. If you play, you may lose the muscle control in your right hand. For life. I order you to completely abstain from piano playing for at least three months.

Curtain closes.

LIEUTENANT: In spite of the doctors' warning, the pianist decided to play. And he did. But during the concert blood poured from his finger, and toward the end the keys were covered in blood. Another aspect of Paderewski's character was revealed he was a fighter. He would never give up. Never...

♪ *Suddenly, a loud sound of a whistle is heard outside, followed by the military band playing a march. The Sergeant runs in.*

SERGEANT: General alarm! General alarm! Fall in on the assembly ground in full battle gear immediately! Move out now! Now!

LIEUTENANT: We have a rehearsal here, sergeant.

SERGEANT: The rehearsal is over, sir. The commander's order. General alert. Last drill prior to departing for Europe.

LIEUTENANT: But Maestro Paderewski's coming tomorrow. The cast members are excused from drills.

SERGEANT: No, sir. They are not excused. Commander's order, sir.

LIEUTENANT: Lieutenant Dygat and I were personally excused by Colonel LePan.

SERGEANT: If you say so, sir. Oh, and all civilians are to leave the camp immediately. *He turns to the Soldiers.* Fall in on the assembly ground. Full gear. Five minutes. Dismissed!

Without a word all six Soldiers grab their gear and run outside followed by the Sergeant. The two Lieutenants and four girls are left confused.

LIEUTENANT: I'm so sorry... and embarrassed... We can't continue the rehearsal tonight. Please, come tomorrow in the afternoon. I'll try to arrange another rehearsal just before the show.

WOMAN 1: If there'll be a show at all.

LIEUTENANT: We'll perform tomorrow. I give you my word.

WOMAN 2: You don't have the final say here, lieutenant, I'm afraid.

LIEUTENANT: I'll convince the colonel. He wants the Maestro's reception to be royal. And what better way to entertain an artist than with art?

WOMAN 3: I don't think we are going to perform. Let's go.

MARY: I hope we will! Can't we at least practice our dances and songs now?

LIEUTENANT: Why not? Of course! Lieutenant Dygat, will you play?

LIEUTENANT DYGAT: Sure. *He sits at the piano.*

LIEUTENANT: What do you want to practice?

WOMAN 1: This song we have in the scene where we welcome the Maestro to Buffalo, you know, when he comes to visit our local Polonia, and a huge crowd meets him at the railway station... "War, o War..."

LIEUTENANT: All right. Dygat, did you get that? Go!

♪ *Lieutenant Dygat plays piano and girls begin the dance and sing.*

Sergeant appears and shouts, interrupting the song.

SERGEANT: I said, all civilians must immediately evacuate the camp. I've checked with the colonel. No one is excused from the drill. The lieutenants must immediately report to their units. It's an order. This is a military camp and we are at war, sir.

He exits.

LIEUTENANT: I am so sorry. But orders are orders.

All girls prepare to leave.

LIEUTENANT DYGAT: This way. I'll accompany you to the gate.

LIEUTENANT: *To Mary* Could you stay a moment?

MARY: Me? Why?

LIEUTENANT: Yes, you, Mary, please, stay one moment... *To Lieutenant Dygat*: Please, take them to the checkpoint... Go!

Lieutenant Dygat and three girls leave. Mary stays behind.

Pause.

LIEUTENANT: We never had a chance to speak alone. Your name is Mary, am I right?

MARY: And we are not going to have that chance now. Yes, I'm Mary. I have to hurry. The sergeant is going to arrest me.

LIEUTENANT: I can't wait to tell you...

MARY: I'd like to hear it. But not now...

LIEUTENANT: Yet, please... I have a feeling that they will cancel the play tomorrow... and we may never meet again. "O, think'st thou we shall never meet again?"

MARY: You speak in verse to me?

LIEUTENANT: So, I have to tell you now... When I saw you for the first time dancing... That radiant smile of yours...

MARY: My smile?

LIEUTENANT: "The brightness of your cheek would shame the stars..."

MARY: You're a poet...

LIEUTENANT: I'm only quoting Shakespeare... "Romeo and Juliet."

MARY: I'm not Juliet.

LIEUTENANT: For me, you are.

MARY: I...?

They hold their hands. They are about to kiss, but they don't do it.

MARY: I have to run, now. You have to report to your unit. It's war time. We'll talk more when it's over.

LIEUTENANT: After the war? I don't know if I will return from the battlefields.

MARY: No, when the drill's over. Or rather tomorrow, after the play. If we do play it...

They kiss delicately.

LIEUTENANT: Now, we must. Please, come tomorrow. Bring your friends. Now we have to hurry.

They exit.

SCENE 3

♪ *Next day. Military band plays a march. Soldiers hang a sign over the gate* "Welcome Maestro Paderewski."

Colonel LePan appears at his desk and Sergeant Cox at his. Lieutenant Chwalski enters and salutes.

LIEUTENANT: Lieutenant Chwalski, sir. As you ordered, sir.

COLONEL: Right. At ease. You were late for the general alarm. You prepared a show that ridicules Maestro Paderewski. You solicited permission for women to enter the military installation. You used a theater rehearsal to cover up your improper behavior. That is, let me be blunt, to cover your amorous affairs. Enough for a court martial. Which you will have. For now, you're under house arrest. You're confined to the quarters. Dismissed.

LIEUTENANT: Sir. May I say something, sir?

COLONEL: Be quick. The Maestro's expected any minute.

LIEUTENANT: Sir, indeed, I was late for the alarm, because, first, I thought that I had been excused, and, second, I had to escort one of the artists to the gate. As for the show, I vehemently reject the charge that it ridicules the Maestro. Whose opinion is this? You, sir, you did not see the show, although I invited you to the last rehearsal and previously offered you the script for review. My private relationships have nothing to do with the service, and I ask you respectfully, sir, not to listen to any unfounded gossip about me.

COLONEL: All right. You'll surely be disciplined for your tardiness. That's military routine. The show is a graver matter. Is this true that you presented Maestro Paderewski as a puppet? We have a witness.

LIEUTENANT: Nobody saw the show.

COLONEL: Sergeant Cox!

Sergeant Cox stands at his desk.

Did you see the Maestro presented as a puppet?

SERGEANT: Yes, sir. I did. A puppet. Redhair. Very funny.

COLONEL: Thank you, sergeant. *Sergeant sits back.* Did you hear it, lieutenant? You wanted to ridicule, to discredit, to offend the Maestro, our great leader and benefactor. He not only convinced president Wilson to permit this Polish army to organize, but he's constantly looking after its welfare, just this week he bought 22,000 gas masks for us with his personal check.

♪ *The telephone rings. The Colonels picks it up.*

COLONEL: Yes, general. We are ready, sir. Thank you, sir.

He puts down the telephone.

COLONEL: General Davis called from the customs post at the bridge over the Niagara river. They are on their way from Buffalo. Maestro Paderewski, Madame Paderewski, their retinue, and three cars full of the international press. They'll be here in about twenty minutes. What did you want to tell the press, lieutenant, with your show? What did you want to tell the world!? That Maestro is a not a person, but a puppet? A puppet of the American government, perhaps? A puppet of the American Polish community? Or even a puppet of the enemy? Some puppet? It's horrifying. Paderewski's a puppet! For heaven's sake, man, do you understand what you're doing?

LIEUTENANT: Sir, it was not a puppet. It was a marionette. A noble and ancient artistic means of expression. Sir, the classical Greek theater presented characters as marionettes. Their actors in stiff costumes and masks, wearing the onkos and cothurnus, looked like huge marionettes. The marionette is known in many highly artistic Asian theater forms. Recently the visionary reformer of theater in Europe, the famous Englishman, Gordon Craig, called for the restoration of the marionette to the stage in order to elevate theater to the highest realm of art...

COLONEL, *interrupting*: What? What's all this about? Have you gone mad, poet? What do the Greeks, the Asians, and that Brit fellow, Braig or Graig, have to do with the show you are putting on here, in Niagara-on-the Lake? I don't have time for your confabulations. Official visit in any minute! Tell me did— you present the Maestro as a puppet? Yes or no?

LIEUTENANT: No, not a puppet. A marionette.

COLONEL: Doesn't make any difference to me. So, you admit it. And your love affair? Do you deny that you kissed a woman in the barracks?

LIEUTENANT: Sir. My officer's honor does not permit me to...

COLONEL: Sergeant Cox!

Sergeant Cox stands at his desk.

COLONEL: We have a witness to that too. He saw it by the window. So, do you deny it?

LIEUTENANT: No.

COLONEL: Here we have it. This woman could be a spy. Not so long ago the French executed a woman named Mata Hari, a German spy. Who knows what this one here was after. This woman could be... a woman. We're going to arrest her if she appears at the camp gate. Dismissed.

LIEUTENANT: You've ordered to arrest her, sir?

COLONEL: Indeed. She'll be arrested, interrogated, put in jail, she'll testify at your court martial, and then she'll be tried herself. Dismissed, I said.

LIEUTENANT: Sir. One last word, sir?

COLONEL: Last word.

LIEUTENANT: Sir...

At this moment two armed soldiers bring Mary, in handcuffs, to the office.

COLONEL: What's this?

SOLDIER 1: Sir, we arrested this woman at the gate, as ordered. She says that she came for the rehearsal, or something. Here she is, sir.

COLONEL: Right. Put her here. And take off those handcuffs. Dismissed.

Soldiers unlock the cuffs and leave.

COLONEL, *suddenly polite*: I am sorry for the handcuffs, but this is the procedure. Sergeant, a chair! *Sergeant brings his own chair.* Sit down, please.

MARY: Thank you, sir. You are very kind, sir. May I ask, sir, why I was arrested?

COLONEL: Yes, of course. That is, no. That is, yes. Pardon the old soldier, but I must be blunt. There are witnesses who say that you made love with an officer in the barracks.

MARY: Oh, Lord. It's a lie.

LIEUTENANT: Sir, I protest!

COLONEL: Shut up, lieutenant. I am sorry, miss, but time is short. So, you deny it? Could you tell me what you were doing in the barracks and what is the nature of the relationship between you and the lieutenant here present?

LIEUTENANT: Sir, what a faux pas! To ask a lady such a question...

COLONEL: I did not ask you for your opinion, lieutenant. *After a pause.* Sergeant! Tell the officers that the Maestro, General Davis, and their party are coming. They'll arrive in about fifteen minutes. The troops must be ready.

SERGEANT: Yes, sir. *He leaves.*

COLONEL: Now, miss, I want to hear from you.

MARY: Sir, I'm going to answer your question. But first...

COLONEL: Of course, but be brief. Duty calls, that is, Maestro Paderewski will be arriving any moment.

MARY: Sir, lieutenant Chwalski is a great poet, and a wonderful playwright too, and a smart director. His piece about the Maestro's life was fast running and funny...

COLONEL: I know. There was a funny puppet ridiculing the Maestro. Could you get to the point, please.

MARY: Yes. The lieutenant presented the Maestro as a marionette, because, he said, no actor in the world would dare to play such a great personality as the Maestro. It was so clever! Entertaining and awesome. It worked perfectly in the first act. Then, in the second part of the show we, the soldiers and the girls from Buffalo and the villages around here... We were telling stories about the Maestro... The stories we learned from our grandparents and parents, and the ones we knew ourselves. Lieutenant Chwalski took down our stories and rewrote them. He gave them such a beautiful expression.

When I was telling my story I could not help but cry. I heard it from my father, a second-generation American, born here, he barley spoke Polish. He went to a concert the Maestro was giving

in Buffalo. Listening to the Maestro playing Chopin, my father started to realize he was still a Pole, that this music, took him back home, to the old country. It was like Chopin infused the pianist's hands with his love of his motherland, Poland, and Paderewski was giving that love back, to my father, to all the Poles in the audience, as a daily bread, sharing with them this great, sacrificial, mystical love. Chopin's love to Poland multiplied by Paderewski's love to Poland...

And after the concert, after round after round of applause, the Maestro stood up and gave a speech on the present predicament of Poland suffering under the oppression of three voracious neighborsÄRussia, Germany and AustriaÄand he said that Poland must be resurrected, and that America should make this resurrection possible, and all Americans, and first of all, all Americans of Polish descent, must give their hearts, money, and, if necessary, blood for the Polish cause.

Sir, my father was carried away. The whole public stood up and clapped and clapped. They chanted Paderewski's name.

Sir, my two brothers and my two cousins are your soldiers. They heard Paderewski's call for a Polish Army and they joined up. I also want to give what little I have to my country, out of my love to the Maestro. And lieutenant John Chwalski too... He wrote that play and directed it out of sheer love for Poland and for the Maestro...

COLONEL: Did you have a monologue like that, indeed? Did others speak with love and respect about the Maestro from the stage? I thought, that is, I was told, that there was only this comic puppet show.

MARY: No. The first part was funny yet full of reverence. The second part was serious and moving. But the last rehearsal was interrupted by the general alert and whoever saw the show saw only the first part.

COLONEL: I see...

MARY: Sir, may I say something more?

COLONEL: Yes, please.

MARY: Sir, you asked me what was the nature of the relationship between myself and the

lieutenant. I can tell you that, sir. I love him, sir. I do.

LIEUTENANT: Mary... You never told *me* that...

SERGEANT *runs in*: Sir, Maestro Paderewski is here! The cars are approaching the checkpoint.

COLONEL: Coming! *To lieutenant:* Lieutenant Chwalski, join your unit for the welcome parade. After the parade you'll make final preparations for your show. I'll come with the Maestro to see it after dinner, as scheduled.

LIEUTENANT: Sir?

COLONEL: It's an order. *To Mary*: If that officer returns from Europe after the war and if you're willing to wait for him, I offer to be a witness at your wedding. Off we go, sergeant.

SERGEANT: Congratulations, sir!

All run out; Lieutenant Chwalski and Mary stay behind.

/LIEUTENANT: You told the colonel that you love me. You only wanted to save my skin, didn't you? Thank you anyway. It was kind of you. Of course, you did not mean it...

MARY: I did mean it.

LIEUTENANT: Truly? Do you mean it now?

MARY: I do. But *you* didn't tell me if you do...

LIEUTENANT: I do... I do. From ever till ever.

They kiss delicately.

MARY: Ever? At least until the end of the war. I will be waiting for you.

LIEUTENANT: I shall return.

They kiss passionately.

I'll be late for the Maestro's welcoming.

They kiss again and run out.

♪ *Military band plays a march. Soldiers in gas-masks stand in "Present Arms" position. Two of them hold a banner "Thank you for the gas-masks, Maestro." Girls join them clapping and waving.*

♪ *Suddenly all lights fade and only one spot is focused on the piano. Lieutenant Dygat comes to the piano and plays Chopin's Etude No.12 in C minor, Op. 10 in its full length. At the end of the piece lights fade out.*

≡ ∫∫∫ ≡

PART 2

Cracow, Poland, June 30, 1941, late evening.

A projection of the panoramic view of the city of Cracow with an inscription

Kraków, Poland, 1941.

A living room in a house in Kraków: A piano (Steinway) covered by blankets, several armchairs, chairs, bookcases, a table, and a dresser.

A gate to the garden with a mailbox.

A fragment of the sidewalk and a street sign Ulica Królowej Jadwigi. Dzielnica Bielany. Kraków

SCENE 1

In the darkness the Gestapo Agent, standing under the street sign, lights a match. He checks a notebook, then, using the same match, he lights a cigarette. We hear aircraft-bombers flying overhead. This sound will be repeated several times during the first scene.

♪ *Professor Dygat plays piano—Paderewski's Menuet in G-major, Op. 14, No. 1. The sound is soft because it is dulled by the blankets. Agent exits.*

Danuta appears at the gate and checks the mailbox. She picks up a note, reads it, takes it with her, and exits. Knocking at the door is heard: three knocks, a pause, and again three knocks. The Professor doesn't hear it, so the knocking is repeated several times. Zofia opens the door. Danuta enters. They hug.

DANUTA: Everything's all right? I hope I'm not late? Nobody's here?

ZOFIA: Nobody. You're the first.

DANUTA: I heard there were mass round-ups from the people running out of the city center. I came on foot from my suburb to yours avoiding downtown. The Germans are cooking up something big again. These bombers are continually flying to the east. Wave after wave.

ZOFIA: They fly to Russia. I heard on the radio that Germans are making rapid progress. They overwhelmed the whole of Europe, now they beat the Soviets.

DANUTA: Not long ago they were friends. *Pause. They listen to the aircrafts.* I'm afraid for the rest of the cast and the director.

ZOFIA: They'll come. God is merciful. Let me take the "Safe Entry" note back to the mailbox for the next arrivals. I'll be back.

She takes the note from Danuta and goes outside. She appears at the gate, looks around, and puts the note in the mailbox. In the meantime Danuta goes to the piano and speaks to the Professor.

DANUTA: Paderewski? Now only Paderewski?

PROFESSOR *stands up and hugs her*: Yes, Paderewski.

♪ *He returns to the piano and begins a new piece, this time Paderewski's Cracovienne fantastique, Op. 14, No.1.*

DANUTA: Only him? Why?

Professor doesn't answer. He only smiles. Zofia returns.

During the following scene the Agent returns to the mailbox.

He opens it, reads the note and puts it back. He exits.

ZOFIA: What is going on in the city?

DANUTA: I don't know. Perhaps they are taking more hostages? Or hunting people down for slave labor in Germany? It's frightening.

♪ *Pause. Machine gun shots are heard in the distance.*

ZOFIA: Another street execution?

DANUTA: Or a skirmish with Home Army combatants?

♪ *They listen. More machine gun shots. Silence. Professor plays all the time.*

ZOFIA: People are dying... somewhere...

DANUTA: And professor is playing piano... In the midst of all this...

ZOFIA: My husband refused to accept the fact that we are at war, that the country is occupied by the Germans and the Soviets, that the Music Academy is closed, that many of his colleagues and students have been arrested, sent to Auschwitz, killed. He almost stopped speaking. He gives private lessons, which allows us to keep going, and he spends all the rest of his time at the piano, playing Paderewski. It's an obsession. He keeps saying that Paderewski's music is the ultimate expression of the Polish soul and the Polish love of the mother country. He says that Paderewski served Poland by serving music and served music by serving Poland.

♪ *They both listen to the music.*

By playing Paderewski, my husband thinks, he carries the torch.

DANUTA: Paderewski? He's in America, so far away. How can he help us here?

ZOFIA: By playing Paderewski—he brings him home—my husband says.

DANUTA: So, he lives in his own world. Good for him.

ZOFIA: But I am worried that one day the outer world will invade his inner world. This will be the end of the whole world for both of us.

DANUTA: You live on a small, quiet street. They aren't looking for the Home Army in such places.

ZOFIA: A German patrol might hear the piano. We put a few blankets over it to dull the sound, but still, someone may overhear. There are Gestapo agents wandering everywhere. And recently we have had so many guests...

DANUTA: Perhaps we should move our rehearsals to someone else's house? What we do is absolutely forbidden. I'd hate to endanger you. If the Germans broke in on a rehearsal or, even worse, a show, everybody would be arrested. Prison, interrogation, torture... If not death... Auschwitz not far...

ZOFIA: We want to be part of the resistance at least in this modest way—to allow an underground theater company to rehearse and perform in our living room. Such a minute contribution. Some fight with guns. You use words. We give you shelter.

Pause.

DANUTA: Nobody's coming.

Pause.

ZOFIA: They'll come. We have to trust. God *is* merciful.

Pause.

Do you want tea? There's no real tea, of course, but I have some delicious herb tea.

DANUTA: Thank you, with pleasure.

ZOFIA: I'll fetch you a cup.

♪ *Zofia leaves. Danuta approaches the Professor, who is still softly playing piano.*

During the following lines we see Mieczysław and Hala arriving at the gate. Mieczysław checks the message in the mailbox, takes it, and they go to the door.

DANUTA: Professor Dygat... Professor... *The Professor doesn't answer and continues playing piano.* Professor... Only Paderewski? And what about Chopin?

♪ *We hear the secret knocking. Danuta goes to the door but is unable to open it. Zofia emerges from the kitchen and opens the door. Enter Mieczysław and Hala, both shaky. Hala in tears.*

ZOFIA: Thank God, you've made it. What happened?

Without a word Mieczysław leads Hala to an armchair. He knees in front of her and holds her hands in his. He turns to the others.

MIECZYSŁAW: Something terrible happened. Olek was killed.

ZOFIA: Oh, my God.

DANUTA: When? Why? What happened?

MIECZYSŁAW *to Hala*: Tell them. Tell them everything. They must know. And the professor, too.

He goes to Professor Dygat, gently puts his hands over the keys of the piano which interrupts Professor playing. Professor, please, listen. You have to hear this. Your best student was killed. Olek was killed.

♪ *Professor looks at him and—without a word—stands up, grabs the blankets and pulls them off the piano. He opens the cover of the piano, returns to his stool and starts playing Paderewski's Variations and Fuga in E flat minor, Op 23. The sound is very loud. The Gestapo Agent appears on the street and listens. Mieczysław, joined by Zofia and Danuta, run to stop the Professor. Zofia hugs him. Mieczysław shuts the piano cover. Danuta puts the blankets back on it. The Agent disappears. All turn to Hala as she begins to speak in a monotonous, lifeless voice.*

HALA: I was a few steps from him lying in a pool of blood. At first it was a small, narrow stream slowly making its way on the stones of the street, coming from under his body, for he fell on his face, the blood must have been pouring out of his stomach. Gradually the stream formed a pool, that pool grew. I was hypnotized by how fast it grew. I could not move. No, I could, I felt that I had to, but I was afraid. I knew that if I moved they would shoot me too, so I remained frozen, motionless, when he was dying there, within my reach, dying, because that blood was still pouring out, and—I saw it with my very eyes—his fingers were making small movements, as if he was scratching the stones, or as if he was delicately touching the keys of the piano.

She interrupts. Then, she speaks loud almost hauling out the words.

No, no, no, don't tell me that I am not guilty. I am. I did not stop his bleeding. I did not protect him. I did not help him.

She bursts in tears. Zofia and Danuta go to her and try to comfort her.

♪ *A new wave of airplanes is flying over.*

ZOFIA: Please, that's enough. Be quiet. Please...

HALA: *She now speaks as absent, but gradually with more energy.* No. I have to tell you how it happened. We were on our way to the rehearsal, here. We were crossing the Matejko Square, part of the crowd on a late afternoon... A throng of people returning home from work, rushing to do some last-minute shopping, taking themselves to their homes, streetcar stops, the railroad station... We were around the place where the Grunwald Victory Monument stood, the old glory of Poland carved in marble and iron, before the Germans blew it up, because it was a memorial of their defeat.

Olek said, "What a coincidence. We are passing the Grunwald Victory Monument, raised by Paderewski, going to professor Dygat, Paderewski's student." And then he said, "Look Hala, there's an empty spot where the monument stood and I wonder how long it will take for the two of us to rebuild it."—"The two of us?" I asked.—"Yes," he smiled, "because there are two things which are guaranteed in my life. One, that the two of us will be together for ever," you know, we married only three months ago, "and second, that we will rebuild this monument after the war."—"After the war?" I asked.—"Are we going to live to see the end of the war?"—"Yes," he burst out. "It'll end soon. We'll win. And we'll rebuild this monument. The whole country."

At that moment we noticed that passers-by were not longer rushing in all directions. Suddenly a wave of people running from the opposite side of the square stopped us. People were running towards us and screaming: "Turn back, turn back, the Germans are closing the square, they're rounding-up people!" We immediately turned and started running the opposite way. But a moving row of uniforms and machine guns appeared in front of us. There were dogs too, barking like mad. We stopped with others, helpless. All the streets were closed. We were trapped.

The lights fade out and only one spot remains on Hala.

♪ *We hear dogs barking and German soldiers screaming*:

"Halt! Halt"—"Hände hoch!"— "Schnell! Schneller!"—"Alle raus! Raus!"

The soldiers and some plainclothes agents quickly broke the crowd into several sections, beating, kicking, pushing, and put them up against walls of the surrounding the square buildings. They ordered us to keep our hands up. Then, they started to systematically check everyone's identity documents, one by one, one by one, selecting some, for no obvious reason, and leading those selected to the side streets where the trucks were waiting to swallow up the arrested. They packed people like cattle. Dogs were yapping, children were screaming, Germans were yelling. Pandemonium.

I stood with Olek near the corner of a street closed by a row of soldiers, but behind them the street looked empty and not far away there was an intersection with another street. We were helplessly waiting for the approaching officers. I had a good, of course forged, document stating that I am an employee of the city hall, and should not be detained in any circumstances, and I knew that Olek had a similar one.

Suddenly he whispered in my ear "I have a gun with me. We were scheduled to have a night action just after the rehearsal." I was petrified. A gun found on him meant immediate death. He whispered again "I'll outsmart them." He smiled. "Stay put. If something happens, you don't know me. Remember. Promise." My heart started to pound like a bell. "I promise." I whispered. He saw how pale I was and he added, these were his last words "I'll see you at the rehearsal."

I suddenly felt like fainting, was it my early pregnancy? I don't know. I started to pray desperately for him. The Gestapo were close. They approached me first. I pulled out my I.D. An officer examined it for a long time and returned it to me without a word. I was free. He moved to Olek. And after that it's like a slow motion silent movie.

♪ *Sound effects stop.*

Olek lowers his right hand to his chest as he was reaching for his I.D. He puts his hand in the pocket. He pulls it out and his hand holds a gun. He shoots the Gestapo officer in his chest. The German's body shakes and his face looks like he is trying to swallow something which he could not swallow. He starts to fall down. Olek immediately turns back and sneaks behind the row of soldiers closing the street. They had not expected anybody to try to flee and before they turn and start to shoot at him, he makes it to the corner of the intersection and disappears down a side street. Thank God.

The very next second or two I heard shots, one, one, then a series, another series, and he appeared again moving backwards, already wounded, and from that side street, his escape route, a group of soldiers emerged shooting at him with machine guns.

DANUTA: We heard these shots even here.

HALA: I saw his body jerked by the bullets. His gun slipped from his hand. And he slowly fell on the pavement. He contracted his body, pulling his knees and elbows toward his stomach, like an embryo. The soldiers stopped shooting. Silence. He relaxed, prone on his face. And that blood started to flow out. His blood. I felt as it was my blood. But no, it was his. I am still alive. I did not move. I did not help him. Why?

♪ *Another wave of bombers.*

DANUTA: How could you? They would have shot you too. And your baby. You have to live.

HALA: Without him?

♪ *Lights return to normal. Professor starts playing, this time very softly, Paderewski's Variations and Fuga in E flat minor, Op 23. Zofia brings a glass of water for Hala. Mieczysław speaks with Danuta aside.*

MIECZYSŁAW: After making the arrests they ordered some men to carry Olek's body to a truck. We'll never even know where his grave is. We can't have a rehearsal tonight.

DANUTA: Naturally. Besides, Karol didn't come either. I'm so worried about him. Was he was arrested in the same round-up?

ZOFIA: I'll take the "Safe Entry" note to the mail-box for him.

MIECZYSŁAW: He will not come.

ZOFIA: So no one else is expected. Why won't Karol come?

MIECZYSŁAW: He wasn't arrested. He's safe.

DANUTA: What happened?

MIECZYSŁAW: I'll tell you at the right time.

DANUTA: Conspiracy secrets? But tell me at least if he is going to play in our new production?

MIECZYSŁAW: No.

DANUTA: Is he leaving our theater?

MIECZYSŁAW: He has left.

DANUTA: The most talented actor of the company. You really can't tell me what happened?

MIECZYSŁAW: No. I am sorry. I'll tell everybody soon. But not today.

DANUTA: Well. On the same day we lost our two leads. I'm afraid we'll have to close our theater.

MIECZYSŁAW: Close the theater?

DANUTA: How are we going to replace our two best actors? It's the end.

MIECZYSŁAW: We will find replacements. The show must go on.

DANUTA: I don't know. There's no hope.

MIECZYSŁAW: This is our way to win this war. It's our duty to keep the theater alive. In spite of deaths, difficulties, threats, and most of all against our own weakness.

DANUTA: You're a naive idealist.

MIECZYSŁAW: No. I am a strong believer. I believe that in these times of bondage art has the power to set us free. Us, and our spectators too. That's why we must do theater. We must.

DANUTA: Words against bullets?

MIECZYSŁAW: Yes. This is our weapon. The word is the emblem of the spirit. The spirit will prevail the barbarism. Beauty...

Zofia suddenly stands up and interrupts.

ZOFIA: It's already nine. Time for the evening news. The curfew is at ten. You must all go soon. Zygmunt, come, listen to the news.

♪ *She goes to the dresser and opens a secret hiding container in it. All, except Hala, approach the dresser. A radio appears. Zofia turns it on. We hear a short fragment of a military march and the characteristic signal of B.B.C. from London "Bum, bum, bum, bum." It is repeated several times. Then we hear:*

"Twenty hours, Greenwich Mean Time. From London, this is the B.B.C. Evening news. Last night, June 29, 1941, at 11.45 PM, Ignacy Paderewski had died in his apartment in the Buckingham Hotel in New York."

♪ *The news shocks all present, while the broadcast continues.*

"Paderewski was a world renowned pianist and composer, statesman and diplomat, leader of the American Polish community, and the highest political and moral authority of the Polish nation. The Poles in Poland and throughout the world mourn his passing and pay him tribute. The Polish Government in Exile in London held a special session in honor of Paderewski, who was President of the Council of Ministers of Poland in 1919. The American President Roosevelt issued a special proclamation emphasizing the invaluable contribution of Paderewski to the Allies victory in World War I and to establishing peace after it. President Roosevelt also decided to bestow on Paderewski the honor of a military funeral and burial at the Arlington National Cemetery. The heads of states of the Allied nations are sending condolences to the Polish Government. The representatives of American Polonia are expressing their deepest sorrow. This is the B.B.C. from London. News continues. The armed conflict between Germany and the Soviet Union is now in its ninth day. The Germans are reported to making rapid advances on all fronts. They use their superior air power and..."

♪ *Zofia turns off the radio. All remain silent. Another wave of bombers.*

DANUTA: This is our third loss today. How can we make up for this one? I quit.

HALA: No. We will stand tall. Against all odds.

♪ *After a while she starts humming "The March of the Falcons." The Professor goes to the piano and accompanies her. Gradually all create a circle and join in the song. While they are singing in soft voices, the Gestapo Agent appears at the street sign and listens. Lights fade out.*

SCENE 2

Three months later. Night. The faint sound of a propeller airplane somewhere high above. Anti-

aircraft search lights appearing and combing the sky. Anti-aircraft gun fire and air-raid sirens are heard.

In his living room professor Dygat plays piano Paderewski's Tatra Album, Op. 12, No. 1. The airplane sound slowly fades out. Professor Dygat continues playing. Blackout. Music fades off.

SCENE 3

A day later. Cracow's panorama projected on the screen. Around the table in the living room sit Colonel Chwalski, Mieczysław, Zofia, Danuta, Hala (her pregnancy is visible), and three new characters Barbara, Bogdan, and Leon. Professor Dygat sits in an armchair near the piano, with notes on his lap. He flaps the pages and, from time to time, he moves his hands as conducting an orchestra.

♪ *From a distance we hear a German military band playing marches. This sound will be a constant background for few first minutes.*

MIECZYSŁAW: I am opening the meeting. *To Collonel* Sir, I welcome you cordially, as an honorable guest. Yet, please, allow us first to cover the theatre business.

COLONEL: Of course. It will be for me an interesting lesson, demonstrations how the conspiracy in the country works.

MIECZYSŁAW: Thank you very much. First then, Barbara, Bogdan, and Leon submitted their requests to become members of our theatre. If accepted, they will be sworn-in. Two active members must introduce a new member. Barbara is sponsored by Zofia and Hala. Zofia, do you recommend Barbara, here present, to be accepted and sworn?

ZOFIA: I do recommend her. I have known Barbara for years. I know her parents too. They are both teachers and good people. Barbara began acting just before the war in the Słowackiego Theater. She performed only one small role before the theater was closed. She is talented, focused, hard-working. I hope she'll be an asset to our company. As a person she is reliable and honest. I recommend her.

MIECZYSŁAW: Hala?

DANUTA *interrupting*: Do we really need this funny ritual...

MIECZYSŁAW: We do. And it's not funny. Hala, do you recommend Barbara?

DANUTA: Childish...

HALA: Barbara is a close friend. We were at the same high school. We can count on her. I trust her. I recommend her.

MIECZYSŁAW: Thank you. Bogdan is sponsored by Danuta and myself. Danuta, do you recommend Bogdan, here present, to be accepted and sworn?

DANUTA: I'd rather abstain.

MIECZYSŁAW: Bogdan told me that you're going to recommend him.

DANUTA: Must we replace the lost friends so hastily?

MIECZYSŁAW: So, you refuse to let Bogdan join the company?

DANUTA: Why such strong words? I'm simply not ready for the changes in the company... Besides, it makes me laugh... All these formalities, all these...

MIECZYSŁAW: Bogdan, I'm sorry. You have to leave the meeting.

HALA: I don't understand you, Danuta. I know Bogdan well. I can...

BOGDAN: Thank you, Hala. But, if I'm not wanted... I'll go...

MIECZYSŁAW: Stay. Hala, do you recommend Bogdan?

HALA: I do. I know Bogdan as a good actor and a reliable friend. Before the war he was a member of the Old Theater acting company and, even young, he played several leads. He was beloved by his colleagues and the public. We need him in our ensemble. I trust him.

DANUTA: I trust him too. But I question...

MIECZYSŁAW: I preside over the meeting, Danuta. I'll let you speak later. I am Bogdan's second sponsor. I have known him for a long time, indeed, since his early youth. He has always shown honesty and care for others. I do recommend him. Leon is sponsored by Zofia and myself. Zofia, do you recommend Leon, here present, to be accepted and sworn?

DANUTA: Here we go again...

ZOFIA: Yes, I do. Leon is my husband's piano student, from the same master-class as Olek... He is hard working. Always prepared. Besides Olek, he was Zygmunt's best student. I never heard any complaint about his conduct. I recommend him.

MIECZYSŁAW: Thank you. I am Leon's second sponsor. I met him just a year ago, when we were already at war. We met, so to speak, underground. The circumstances are of a sensitive character, so I will not disclose them. I have found him serious and courageous. I do recommend him. Does anybody have any questions for the sponsors or to the candidates? *Silence.* Danuta? You may speak now.

DANUTA: What about? This is sickening.

MIECZYSŁAW: Is that all you wanted to say?

Danuta doesn't answer.

Anybody else? *Silence.* We're going to proceed then. Barbara, Bogdan and Leon—stand up and raise your right hands.

Barbara, Bogdan, and Leon follow instructions and then repeat after Mieczysław. Danuta raises her hand too and waves it, but Mieczysław doesn't pay attention to her.

MIECZYSŁAW: I solemnly swear...

BARBARA, BOGDAN, AND LEON: I solemnly swear...

MIECZYSŁAW: To work and fight tirelessly and courageously for the good of my country and for the good of the theater...

BARBARA, BOGDAN, AND LEON: To work and fight tirelessly and courageously for the good of my country and for the good of the theater...

♪ *Suddenly, we hear airplanes flying low over the house. The noise is so laud that people must outshout it.*

MIECZYSŁAW: To obey all the rules of this company, which I know and accept...

BARBARA, BOGDAN, AND LEON: To obey all the rules of this company, which I know and accept...

MIECZYSŁAW: And the orders of the superiors...

BARBARA, BOGDAN, AND LEON: And the orders of the superiors...

MIECZYSŁAW: I also swear to keep strictly all secrets...

BARBARA, BOGDAN, AND LEON: I also swear to keep strictly all secrets...

MIECZYSŁAW: Until death...

BARBARA, BOGDAN, AND LEON: Until death...

MIECZYSŁAW: So help me God.

BARBARA, BOGDAN, AND LEON: So help me God.

MIECZYSŁAW: Congratulations, Barbara. Congratulations, Bogdan. Congratulations, Leon.

They shake hands.

DANUTA *imitating Mieczysław, but, instead of shaking hands, she salutes Barbara, Bogdan, and Leon*: Congratulations, Barbara.

Congratulations, Bogdan. Congratulations, Leon.

MIECZYSŁAW: Danuta! Stop it! It's not enough that the Germans have another victory parade in the city square, this time, after taking Smoleńsk, I guess. Orchestras, tanks, plains, columns of infantry...

♪ *Another group of aircrafts. The noise is deafening. They disappear.*

Does any new member want to say something?

BARBARA: I simply thank you. It's such a joy to be in a theater company again. When my theater was closed by the Germans it was like the whole world ended. Years of training wasted. Great expectations shattered. I loved so much that moment of entering the stage and feeling the warmth of the lights and the delicate breeze coming from the auditorium, full of people, alive, clapping, laughing. I always wanted to give them the very best I had. And suddenly the stage was closed. I'm homeless. I volunteered to tell fairy tales in a children's hospital. For a living, I worked as a nurse's aid. It was like hibernation. And now you offer me the theatre again, even if underground. I am alive again.

DANUTA: I don't know if I'm alive...

♪ *Yet another group of aircrafts.*

MIECZYSŁAW: Bogdan?

BOGDAN: I am an actor, in peace or war. War stopped me from performing. You're giving me a chance to perform. For me the war has ended today. Thank you.

MIECZYSŁAW: It's not so simple. We still have a long way to go before the war is over, or rather, before we bring it to its end.

♪ *At this moment the German military band stops.*

ZOFIA: Finally. I hope that the Germans have finished their parade.

COLONEL: The next one might celebrate their taking of Moscow. The Russians are in constant retreat.

Silence.

LEON: May I say something now?

MIECZYSŁAW: Sure. Wait! Didn't I hear something on the street? Silence, please. *Pause.* No. Go ahead.

LEON: I am aware that I am to replace Olek. It is a great challenge. I promise you to work as hard

as he had and be brave as him. Hala, I swear this directly to you, I will avenge Olek's death. I will...

DANUTA, *interrupting*: I protest. Karol would never tolerate even a thought about revenge. He was always talking about loving our enemies. I didn't understand him, to be frank. Yet, even if he is not with us, we have to respect his point.

BOGDAN: Love the killers?

DANUTA: He was adamant about that. He repeated that killing will not end killing, hate will not stop hate. Only love. Mieczysław, is Karol going to come today?

MIECZYSŁAW: No. But I will tell you something about him. In a while. I think that since our new members have been sworn in, we can proceed with the meeting. I am happy that despite the irreparable losses we suffered, our company survives and even grows. On the agenda we have still two items: one, a welcome to Colonel Chwalski and his talk on Paderewski; two, news about Karol. Then—the rehearsal.

DANUTA, *interrupting*: Can't you say it now, don't let us wait!

MIECZYSŁAW: May I proceed with the agenda? We have a formal meeting.

DANUTA: No! I don't care for your funny formal protocol. If you know something about Karol, just tell us.

MIECZYSŁAW, *to Chwalski*: Colonel, will you agree to move your item of the agenda down?

COLONEL: Sure. I can wait. Oh, and don't call me colonel all the time.

DANUTA: Thank you, colonel... That is, sir... Mieczysław, please tell us about Karol...

MIECZYSŁAW: Karol is safe and in good health. He left the theater because he decided to enter the seminary for priests.

DANUTA: The seminary is closed, like all other schools. Something's wrong here.

MIECZYSŁAW: I won't enter into details, Danuta. But think for a while. Universities, colleges, high schools, and even elementary schools above the fourth grade were shut down by the German and Soviet occupiers. All theaters were closed. But we are preparing shows underground and we perform them in secret. Underground instruction goes on and scores of students continue their studies on all levels. So...

DANUTA: So, he is in a clandestine seminary, yes? Yes?

MIECZYSŁAW: I did not say that.

DANUTA: Come on! Don't you trust us?

MIECZYSŁAW: It's not a matter of trust but of the rules of secrecy. We're playing a very dangerous game underground. Don't forget—any violation is punished by death.

DANUTA: Didn't Karol leave a message for me? That is, for us...? Didn't he tell you to pass something on to me...? He disappeared like a morning fog. Without a word. Without a...

MIECZYSŁAW: He asked me to say hello to everyone...

DANUTA: Say hello?

MIECZYSŁAW: Yes. And to tell that his choice is firm and he is very happy to have made it. He'll keep praying for all of us.

DANUTA: So, we're going to have a chaplain for our theater in a few years.

HALA: He's so smart and hard working that he'll became a bishop, I tell you.

DANUTA, *sarcastically*: Or maybe a pope!

All laugh.

MIECZYSŁAW: May I proceed?

DANUTA: Proceed. According to the rules. *She suddenly stands up and runs to the kitchen, crying.*

MIECZYSŁAW: What's wrong with her?

ZOFIA: You don't know? Men don't notice anything. *She follows Danuta to the kitchen.* I'll be back. *She exits.*

MIECZYSŁAW: Come back as soon as you can, we're going to lose our quorum. In the meantime, I'll proceed. Returning to the agenda. Item number three: Discussion of our next production. Item number four: Other business. Do you accept the agenda?

HALA: Without objections. I'll take minutes.

MIECZYSŁAW: Thank you. Let's proceed. Item three. Welcome to Colonel Chwalski. Colonel, that is, sir... We are very happy that you agreed to meet with us. We heard about you a lot from professor Dygat. So, we are excited to have the opportunity to meet you personally, a hero of the Great War. I am not supposed to disclose anything about your current mission beyond this: Our guest arrived via the sky and a parachute...

Zofia and Danuta return. Mieczysław continues:

The Colonel's first contact in Poland was his old friend and fellow veteran professor Dygat. We're using the Dygats' home for the rehearsals. Thanks to this coincidence we have the privilege of meeting the Colonel. It is indeed an honor. Welcome.

COLONEL: Thank you, Mieczysław. It's good to be in the old country after so many years. Even under the circumstances of war. As you know, Zygmunt, that is professor Dygat and I served together in the Paderewski's Kosciuszko Army in America during the Great War. We were shipped to the battlefields of France, then transported to Poland, where we fought the Bolsheviks. Except for some minor wounds, both of us survived, as you see.

ZOFIA: John, you're not telling them that because of your bravery and military talents you quickly advanced from lieutenant to colonel. Zygmunt stayed a lieutenant...

COLONEL: But after the war Zygmunt became a professor at the famous Music Academy in Cracow while I was a reporter for a Buffalo newspaper and director of theatre at the Mickiewicz Society. After the war, that first war, Zygmunt fell in love in Poland, married a Polish girl, and stayed here. I returned to my Polish girl in America. When the present war began I followed my old ways.

I tried to volunteer for the Polish army. But unlike the Great War, there was no Polish army in America. To make the long story short—I became an aide to Maestro Paderewski when he arrived to America last year. I heard his last speeches. Then, I marched in his funeral.

BARBARA: Colonel... We listen to the B.B.C. from time to time... But we are in the dark... Tell us... Are we going to win this war? The Germans rule over the whole continental Europe and now are beating the Soviets. The Japanese are wining in China. America is still neutral. Will she join? When?

COLONEL: I don't know when. But America will wake up again and tip the scale. As during the first war.

DANUTA: Will America help Poland to resurrect? Paderewski no longer knocks to the American doors for help.

COLONEL: Paderewski's loss is irreparable, for sure. But it is you, who are going to decide the fate of PolandÄyour generation, here, in the country.

MIECZYSŁAW: We know that. Because of this we do theater.

A moment of silence.

HALA: You heard, of course, Colonel, that professor Dygat studied with Paderewski in the thirties in Switzerland.

COLONEL: Of, course, I did.

HALA: But you may not know that Paderewski considered the Professor his best student, he spoke about him as his "adopted son-in-the-piano." My late husband was the Professor's student... A good one...

COLONEL: Your late husband?

MIECZYSŁAW: Hala's husband fell in action three months ago.

COLONEL: Paderewski's "grandson-in-the-piano..."

HALA: Paderewski was my husband's idol, for he combined absolute devotion to music with untiring service to his country. My husband wanted to follow that...

ZOFIA: He was like that.

COLONEL: Paderewski would have been proud of him.

MIECZYSŁAW: Colonel...

COLONEL: Colonel, again?

MIECZYSŁAW: Sir... Would you like to tell us more about Paderewski? You knew him well. You were close to him.

COLONEL: You certainly know from the professor, that it all started when the two of us prepared a production in honor of Maestro at the Kościuszko Army training camp at Niagara-on-the-Lake, near the famous Niagara Falls. It was an awkward and funny show. I represented him, the great master, in the form of a marionette. It was a risky concept. I almost faced a court martial for that. But Maestro loved it. Old story...

Without a word Zofia leaves and after a while returns with a large object covered by a rug and gives it to professor Dygat while Colonel continues.

Zygmunt Dygat played piano in the show. Paderewski found his performance very promising. That prepared the ground for the professor's further studies with the Maestro, later on. But then, in 1918, we went to war. I took the Paderewski marionette with me to France, then to Poland. Zygmunt and I were giving shows for the troops. I'd tell them about Paderewski and operated the marionette, Zygmunt played piano. Of course, if a piano could be found somewhere near the lines...

Professor and Zofia's approach Colonel who interrupts his talk.

ZOFIA: I'm sorry, John, for interrupting... We have a surprise for you. Remember, leaving Poland you left something with Zygmunt...

PROFESSOR: Here...

Zofia unwraps the object and we see the Paderewski marionette— the same as in Act 1.

COLONEL: What a surprise. Marvelous. My old marionette. How did you preserve it?

He starts operating the marionette. He walks it to the piano, sits it on the stool and pretends that the marionette plays piano.

ZOFIA: It was a memento of Zygmunt's first encounter with Paderewski. We guarded that marionette like a treasure. It survived the bombardments...

COLONEL: Thank you. Old times come alive. Zygmunt, what about a concert for four hands?

♪ *Professor takes a chair, moves to the piano, sits down and starts playing Paderewski's Krakoviak Op. 5, No. 1, while Colonel operates the marionette. It looks like two people are playing piano. The Gestapo Agent appears at the street and listens. All present in the living room listen and, when the piece is over, applaud. The Agent goes off. The Colonel walks the marionette to the table, mounts the table, and operates the marionette as if Paderewski was giving a speech.*

COLONEL: Ladies and Gentlemen, you asked me to talk about my life and works. It is a humbling request. I can respond to it only with simplicity, brevity, and truth. First, were twenty-five years of schooling and studies. Next, came twenty-five years of a virtuoso career...

LEON, *gently inserting his comments*: It was a brilliant, astonishing, irresistible, world career. He won attention, respect, and praise from critics and connoisseurs, he inspired the love and adoration of audiences. He became an idol and a celebrity. He played at monarchs' courts and presidents' mansions. He traveled all over the world...

COLONEL: I am aware that my piano performances, as well as my compositions, were favorably accepted by some. I myself knew that I have had to work hard round the clock...

MIECZYSŁAW: Excuse me, for a sec... Silence, please. *He listens.* No... Please, go on...

LEON: His phenomenal technique provided a solid foundation for his personal interpretations, crowned by ecstatic and entrancing play.

COLONEL: To tell the truth, I felt embarrassed many times by the interest I aroused...

LEON: He was a handsome, attractive, tall man; his golden-red hair gave him an unusual look and an aura of angelic beauty. He became the object of a cult, known as "Paddymania..." Once, two young ladies sneaked into his dressing room and, in spite of his desperate resistance, cut of a tuft of his hair...

COLONEL: During the Great War I switched from music to politics. I was elevated to the position of the leader of the Poles in America, and soon after, of all Poles. I returned to Warsaw and became the President of the Council of Ministers of Poland.

LEON: President Wilson once said about him "He conquered America with his music and then he convinced me to restore independent Poland. I thought to myself: If Poland breeds such excellent artists, such great minds, and such hard working people as Paderewski, she certainly deserves to be an equal member of the family of the world's civilized nations."

♪ *Suddenly, we hear alarm sirens and anti-aircraft gun fire. After a while we also hear a faint sound of a propeller airplane somewhere high above—all as at the beginning of scene 2. Anti-aircraft search lights appear and comb the sky.*

COLONEL: A companion for me is coming from England, or what?

♪ *All sounds gradually fade off.*

COLONEL: Let's return to our story. When Poland was resurrected my political objectives were fulfilled and I could return to the piano. But, because of my political duties, I neglected keyboard...

LEON: It was known that, preparing for concerts, Paderewski practiced days and nights, from twelve to sixteen hours at the key board.

COLONEL: I did not give concerts for a long time. My fingers refused to obey me. I was considering quitting music. Yet, I finally I decided to return to the concert halls.

LEON: His first performance, after the long hiatus, took place in Carnegie Hall in New York, November 22, 1922. This concert is described as one of the greatest moments in world music history. A universally respected statesman appeared on the stage. The auditorium rose in respect. Then a virtuoso gave a concert, playing with absolute mastery. Audiences, fellow artists, critics, impresarios, fans—all were enchanted, fascinated, overwhelmed, and enraptured with joy. It was the ultimate victory.

COLONEL: I was humbled by the reception of my performance... I toured again. Most frequently in America, for crowds of thousands and for closed circles of connoisseurs, or at the White House...

LEON: Paderewski played for and befriended all American Presidents of his time: Theodore Roosevelt, Woodrow Wilson, Calvin Coolidge, Franklin Delano Roosevelt...

COLONEL: The attack of Germany and Soviet Union on Poland in 1939, and the outbreak of the new war forced me to return to politics once more. I came to America to again mobilize public opinion in support of my mortally endengered country.

LEON: But an exhausting schedule of meetings, conferences, and speeches was too much for the old man. A "Modern Immortal," as he was called by many, died on June 29, 1941.

Colonel, operating the marionette, performs a pantomime scene: Paderewski walks, speaks, he feels pain in his chest and slowly falls down.

♪ *At the beginning of the pantomime professor Dyga—apparently understanding the Colonel's intentions—plays softly the beginning of Paderewski's Variations' and Fugue in E flat minor, Op. 23.*

Silence.

Zofia goes to the piano and stands at its side.

ZOFIA: Zygmunt knows all Paderewski's works. Zygmunt, please, play the famous *Menuet à l'Antique...*

Professor nods in agreement.

This piece is a summary of the best of Paderewski. It is sad, yet not pitiful; it is noble and elegant; it is light and graceful; it is strong and powerful.

♪ *Professor starts playing the Menuet in G major, Op. 14, No. 1, while Zofia keeps talking. The Agent appears for a moment under the street sign and then walks away.*

ZOFIA: The *Menuet* begins as if someone would test the smoothness of the dance floor with light touches of the foot, once and twice, once and twice. The theme is introduced in the first bars. It is simple, graceful, dancing, melodious. Then, an opposition arises between delicacy, moderation, and restraint—and the temptation to sing loud, dance fast, and explode with unlimited vigor. This is Paderewski! He could not miss an opportunity to run through the keys with wild abandonment and display his amazing technique. At core part, the *Menuet* mutates into an—almost—Chopinian *Mazurka*. The echoes of Chopin wake the echoes of a Polish landscape in early autumn, here and there illuminated by rays of sun, fraught with the mysterious and unutterable Polish nostalgia. The country panorama seems to enlarge and embraces a ballroom in a castle, where airy shadows swirl. But immediately the composition returns to a musical whisper. It poses clouded and enigmatic questions, repeats them and transforms, never answering with any certainty. We are left with the feeling of a mysterious ceremony in a palace of beauty, of which we are allowed only a glimpse as if through a half-open door...

A pause.

COLONEL: Thank you, Zofia! Thank you, Zygmunt!

A pause.

You surprised me with my old marionette. I have a surprise for you too.

From a hidden pocket he pulls up a small tape-player:

See this wonder? The tape and voice recorder. The military has them now. I guess, they'll be in mass productions in twenty years or so. I brought you Paderewski's voice. Listen...

♪ *He pushes the button and Paderewski's voice is heard:*

PADEREWSKI'S VOICE ON THE TAPE. A RECORDING OF PADEREWSKI'S LAST SPEECH SOLICITING POLITICAL AND ECONOMIC HELP FOR POLAND. (THE RECORDING AVAILABLE IN THE INTERNET.)

When the tape is over, the Colonel comments on it.

COLONEL: It's Paderewski's last recorded speech. Even a few days before his death he was pleading for help to his country.

A pause.

Mieczysław, you wanted me to speak. I could go on... But your have to proceed with your meeting...

DANUTA: With the agenda!

MIECZYSŁAW: Thank you, sir, thank you out of my, out of our, hearts. *Suddenly.* Hold on! Leon, check around the house and come back. *Leon immediately goes to the door but he is unable to unlock it. Zofia comes to help him.*

ZOFIA: A lock in the door jams. It doesn't want to open. It's so difficult to get someone to repair things like this these days... Only I know how to operate it...

She opens the door. Leon exits. All wait. Leon returns.

LEON: Nobody.

MIECZYSŁAW: Thanks. Now, back to our agenda...

DANUTA: I told you. The agenda!

MIECZYSŁAW: Sure. Point number four: What to do next? The cast of "King-Spirit" by Słowacki is shattered. Olek... departed... Karol quit... Hala's expecting... We have three new members ready to substitute for them. That's great. But we have to consider also other options, that is, the preparation of other shows.

DANUTA: If we are going to still function at all, which might be impossible...

MIECZYSŁAW: We have to keep going.

DANUTA: If we are going to do anything, we have to revive "King-Spirit" first. We owe this to Olek and Karol. And Hala would be able to perform in it too, after her delivery. She can alternate with Barbara. Am I right, Barb?

BARBARA: Sure. I will gladly take Hala's role and give it back to her when she's ready.

HALA: No, no, we'll perform in turns. One show for you, the next for me.

BOGDAN: I can take the role left by Karol in "King-Spirit", but, perhaps we should do another show. Why not a Shakespeare?

MIECZYSŁAW: Shakespeare? In our theater we focus not on the action but on the text. Not on creating characters but on the delivery of the word in the name of a character. As far as new material is concerned I'm currently working on an adaptation of "Pan Thaddeus" by Mickiewicz.

HALA: Beautiful!

DANUTA: Karol would have played Pan Thaddeus if he had still been with us. Perhaps he'd return if you offer him such a great lead?

MIECZYSŁAW: He has already made his choice.

DANUTA: I'm only joking. *She laughs hysterically. Nobody else laugh. Silence.*

LEON: It seems to me that a revival of "King-Spirit" would be better. It'll be our tribute to Olek and a sort of continuation of Karol's presence in the theater.

MIECZYSŁAW: Any more thoughts? I have another proposal. We heard the Colonel's story on Paderewski. Professor was his student. Olek was, and Leon is, his follower. Both the professor and Leon can play piano in a show. Why can't we prepare a play based on Paderewski's life? Something similar to what the Colonel and the Professor did back then in America. If the Colonel would be so kind to help me, I could come up with an appropriate scenario. Our audiences would love to hear about Paderewski and listen to his music.

LEON: I'm all for it.

DANUTA: I could play Madame Paderewska. After all, who's a star in this company?

BARBARA: He had many female fans and enthusiasts. I could be one of them.

BOGDAN: Will there be a role for me?

MIECZYSŁAW: It depends on the script. Perhaps there shall be a role of Sylvin Strakacz, maestro's faithful personal secretary.

ZOFIA: A play on Paderewski? It's a fine idea. I even have a title for it "Paderewski's Children".

MIECZYSŁAW: Perhaps "Paderewski's Children and Grandchildren"?

ZOFIA: No. "Paderewski's Children". To the point, stronger, and more general as well. It would be about all who recognized Paderewski's spiritual leadership and his artistic mastery.

MIECZYSŁAW: You're right. But first we have to have the play.

COLONEL: I would love to help you. But I won't be staying long in Cracow. I have other orders.

MIECZYSŁAW: I'll ask you only for a few hours. I'll come with a notebook. Or, perhaps, we can use the recorder?

COLONEL: Perfect. This little box can play a voice and can record it.

MIECZYSŁAW: Thank you very much advance.

ZOFIA: I'll put the toy in my safe place.

MIECZYSŁAW: It's settled, then. Other proposals? *He waits a while.* We will revive "King-Spirit" in the near future. We will begin preparations for "Pan Thaddeus". Our next show, however, will be "Paderewski's Children". Is there any other business? *He pauses. Nobody speaks.* All right. I adjourn the meeting.

DANUTA: I adjourn the meeting, too! Thank you all for a productive conference.

MIECZYSŁAW: The curfew is near. We have to be leaving in a hurry. As always, individually, or in small groups. Hala, accompanied by Barbara, you go first. I'll be the last. Colonel, it was an honor to meet you. I'll come back tomorrow to listen to you. Zofia and Zygmunt, thank you for your hospitality.

♪ *Professor goes to the piano and starts playing Paderewski's Mazurka in E minor, Op. 5, No. 2. All hug, shake hands and leave. The Agent observes in the shadows.*

♪ *Blackout. Music fades off.*

SCENE 4

Night. Propelers's sound—as in Scene 2—anti-aircraft guns, sirens, search-lights.

♪*In the leaving room Professor plays Paderewski's Tatra Album Op. 12, No. 1. Noises and lights fade off.*

SCENE 5

Two months later. Late Fall. Afternoon. The panorama of Cracow—as before. Zofia and Professor prepare the room for the show. Zofia is in an evening gown and Professor in a dress coat.

ZOFIA: The opening night!

They take the Polish national flag from the hidden drawer in the dresser and put it on the wall. They rearrange the furniture and bring additional chairs for spectators. The marionette of Paderewski sits i

n the corner of the room. They dialogue during these activities.

ZOFIA: The national flag. A venerated treasure. Prohibited by the enemies. Once, before the war high on a mast in front of the home. Nowadays preserved in a hidden place. In the Paderewski's show it will make a most appropriate set. What else? Zygmunt, could you bring roses from the kitchen?

Professor brings two roses in a flower-pot.

PROFESSOR: Roses. White and red.

ZOFIA: National colors. How many people, I mean, spectators, should we expect? Twenty?

PROFESSOR: Thirty, or so. Mieczysław knows all of them. No written lists, of course.

ZOFIA: If more come, they can sit on the floor. Anything else? All's ready. Although there are no posters around the city, no newspapers' adds, and spectators were invited individually by word of mouth, it's a grand opening. "Paderewski's Children"! I did not write it, but I'm getting credit for the title. The actors should start coming in about an hour. The spectators in about two hours. Why don't we have a cup of tea, while we wait?

♪ *She goes to the kitchen. Professor sits at the piano—covered by blankets—and plays Paderewski's Krakowiak in B flat major, Op. 5, No. 3. The Gestapo Agent appears on the street, listens, and goes off. After a while Zofia returns with tea. She puts one cap on the piano. She sits and sipping tea listens to the music.*

The Agent appears at the mailbox. This time he is accompanied by two Gestapo soldiers in full gear. The Agent checks the note and they go off. Zofia speaks:

I'm so happy that they've prepared that show on Paderewski. The country is completely cut off from any information from abroad, except for illegal radios. Not too many of us have them. The underground press is also a rarity. People are hungry for news. For the theater too. They are going to get both tonight. *A pause.* If only all the actors arrive safely. *A pause.* I hope that the Colonel is safe, somewhere. *A pause.* On an afternoon like this I can almost forget the war, the menace. *A pause.* I feel so secure and happy. *A pause.* The war will end. You'll return to the Academy. Mieczysław and his group will open their theater and perfrom for thousands. I will form a committee for rebuilding the Grunwald Monument. Olek's last wish must be fulfilled. *A pause.* We'll go hiking in the Tatra Mountains again. Quiet and silent. Without the air-raid sirens. *A pause.*

Remember, Zygmunt, our last morning in Paderewski's mansion in Switzerland? Paderewski invited me, the unknown wife of his already famous student, for your final concert after your successful completion of the four stages of his "master class". I remember them so well as if it was me, not you, learning from the master: Perfecting technique, structuring the piece to be played, working on the separate elements, and putting all these elements together, forgetting about them, play in ecstasy, following your emotions and your soul's steers. I learned these stages from your letters. The month long master-class was crowned with a concert in the Maestro's private studio.

It was a calm, joyful, long evening. Both a farewell celebration and an opening of a new era in our life. As Paderewski's favorite student and with his recommendation you were to start an

European piano tour in the fall. I were to travel with you. We were to start in Paris in the Fall of 1939. It did not happened. War broke out. Bombs. Killed. Wounded. Desperate. Horror. *A pause.*

But then, it was still early Spring of 1939. Early morning. We stood on the balcony of the Paderewski's palace looking at the pink and orange patches of snow painted by the rising son on the laces of the Alpine peaks. A delicate fog was brewing at our feet over the Geneva Lake and ascending into the sky in the form of small, disappearing clouds, light like angel feathers. There was something overwhelmingly peaceful and mysterious in nature, in us too. I said, "Let it last." You understood me, and you said. "It will last. From ever till ever."

In that moment we escaped from time. We were only for ourselves. Time ceased to pass, run, fly, to be measured, to vanish, and to confront the past with the future. It stopped. No, it rather merged with eternity. It became a time without time...

♪ *Characteristic secret knocking at the door. Zofia still smiling to his dreams goes to the door.*

Who's here so early?

She goes to the door. She opens. She screams. She raises her hands. The Agent with a gun in his hand appears, followed by two Gestapo soldiers.

AGENT: Shhh... Quiet. No stupid moves, no screaming. Alles wird in Ordnung sein. Go to that chair—*he points out*—sit down and put your hands on your neck. Go! Schnell! *To Professor* Professor, Guten Abend, sir, good evening. Playing Paderewski? Stop it. *Professor interrupts his playing.* Stay there at your stool. Don't move. *He orders the Gestapo soldiers* You! Hier. You, Hier. *He walks around the room.*

Well, well, well... Everything prepared for the show. But there will be no show. The Polish flag. Forbidden. There's no such thing as Poland anymore. Illegal theater production, to make things worse... Chairs for spectators. How many guests do we expect? There's plenty of room in Auschwitz. *He suddenly tears dow the national flag, makes a ball of it, and throws it to Zofia.* Here, put it in your secret drawer along with your radio and recorder.

Zofia catches the flag and systematically folds it on her knees. The Agent picks the roses, a red and a white, from the flower pot. From your own garden? How nice. I like roses. But yours have the wrong colors. *He breaks the roses.* We're going to wait. We'll let everybody in. We'll be hospitable. Yet, nobody will leave alone. We'll wait. *He sees the marionette.*

What a surprise... Maestro Paderewski? Of course, Paderewski. I listened to him in Hamburg, and again in Dresden. He performed Beethoven and List splendidly. Chopin too, but I did not like Chopin. Paderewski. Great pianist. But, unfortunately he turned out an enemy of the Third Reich. Adolf Hitler offered Paderewski the presidency of Poland as a German protectorate. It was one more expression of the Führer's utter generosity and a guarantee of peace for Poland, for Europe, for the world. But the old, stupid, and stubborn man refused. So, he's the enemy. He was, rather. He went to hell along with his lofty ideals.

Professor, play something for me, please.

♪ *Professor begins to play Paderewski's Mazurka in E minor, Op. 5, No. 2.*

No! Not this! I despise these Slavic lunatics Chopin, Paderewski, Opieński, Szymanowski. No, no, not that. Play for me a good German master. Wagner, Beethoven, Handel, Bach. Oh, yes. Bach for me, please. Let's return to healthy German roots.

♪ *Professor starts playing Bach's Italian Concerto.*

Good. I like that. This music is so structured, so clear, so pure, so strict, so orderly.

♪ *He sits and listens while Professor continues to play.*

Danuta, Barbara, Bogdan, Leon and Hala with a baby-carriage appear on the street at the gate. Danuta checks the note in the mailbox. They are about to go to the entrance of the house when Leon stops them.

LEON: Listen... Do you hear what the professor is playing?

DANUTA: He's playing piano, as usual, for hours no end.

LEON: No. It's not that he is playing. It's what he is playing.

DANUTA: What? A piece. Let's go.

LEON: No, no, no. It's Bach. Nowadays professor plays only Paderewski. Never any German composers. Even if he loves them and played them before the war. He was a Bach specialist. No more. And now he's playing Bach's *Italian Concerto*. It's Bach. Definitively Bach.

DANUTA: So what? He changed his repertoire for today.

LEON: No, no. There must be something to it. I don't know what.

BOGDAN: Paderewski or Bach, let's go and see what is going on. The "Safe Entry" note was in its place. The way is open. Let's go.

LEON: Stay. Don't go. It must be something unusual. I'm telling you.

BARBARA: I'll go and find out. You stay and wait. I'll return if everything is all right. If I don't return, don't enter.

HALA: I'll go too. If there's a problem the baby will be my alibi. As I dropped by to a friend to show her the new baby...

BOGDAN: What problem? What problem?

BARBARA: Maybe there's nothing to it. But simply, let's play it safe. I'll go and I'll tell you. *To Hala* You stay. You must be careful for the two of you.

HALA: If I must...

DANUTA: Don't let us wait to long. It's cold.

BARBARA: Sure. I'll be back in a minute.

She takes the "Safe Entry" note from the mailbox, goes to the door and knocks using the secret code. Agent and Zofia stand up. Professor keeps playing.

AGENT: *To Zofia*: Sit down and keep quiet. How nice... We have our first guest.

He pulls the gun out and goes to the door, He wants to open the door but the lock is jammed.

What's that? *To Zofia, whispering* The lock is jammed. You, landlady, be so kind to open. Move! And don't try to play any tricks on me.

Zofia slowly unlocks the door. The Agent brutally moves her to the side. He opens the door. Barbara appears. The Agent whispers to her:

Hände hoch! Hands up. Come in. Shut the door behind you. Welcome. Come in. Close the door behind you, I tell you. The professor might get a cold.

Suddenly Barbara turns and runs away, slamming the door. She disappears. Agent fires and runs after her, followed by Gestapo men, but they are stopped by the closed door which stops their chase. They try to open the lock. Professor stops playing. The Agent forces Zofia to open the lock. Barbara appears at the gate. She is wounded.

BARBARA: Run, run, the Gestapo's inside... Run away...

She collapses. Hala kneels at her side.

Save your baby, please... Run... Leave me...

DANUTA: Oh, no. We'll not leave you... *She helps her stand up.* Here...

BOGDAN: *Takes the note "Safe Entry" and tears it into pieces.* Let's go! Disperse! All directions!

All run away to different directionsÄHala with the baby carriage, Danuta and Leon helping Barbara. Agent and Gestapo men appear.

AGENT: Damn it! Follow them! Fire! We must stop them! Stop! Stop!

All run to different directions. Shooting is heard.

Zofia runs to the hall and returns in a coat, caring Professor's coat.

♪ *Professor looks at her and starts playing Chopin's Etiude No.12, c-moll, Op. 10 (Revolutionary). Zofia slowly takes off the blankets off the piano and opens the cover—the sound bursts. She takes off her coat and throws Professor's coat on a chair. She places Paderewski's marionette on an armchair and sits on another armchair. Smiling, she listens to the music.*

Mieczysław appears at the mailbox and checks for the "Safe Entry" note. He doesn't find it. He looks around, find the pieces of the note on the ground. He quickly exits.

♪ *Lights focus on Professor playing piano.*

Lights fade out.

EPILOGUE

♪ *Professor continues to play.*

Mieczysław, Danuta, Barbara, Bogdan, Leon and Hala appear in the auditorium. Hala holds a five-year old boy by the hand who holds two roses—white and red.

Colonel Chwalski walks Paderewski's marionette in. The marionette listens to the music.

The Soldiers and the Girls (form Part I) surround the marionette. All other actors joins them.

When Professor finishes playing—they applaud him.

The Boy offers the roses to Professor.

Professor takes the Boy by hand leads him to the marionette, gives him the roses and the Boy offers the roses to the marionette.

THE END

Buffalo – Niagara-on-the Lake 2003

PADEREWSKI RETURNS

A PLAY

CHARACTERS
Ignacy Paderewski
Helena Paderewska, his wife
Miss Gloria, owner of "Hotel Paso Robles"
Miss Wonderwrite, music critic
Sylwin Strakacz, Paderewski's personal secretary
Doctor Fronczak
The Mayor of the town Ciężkowice in Poland
Stephen Trojanowski, Paderewski's plenipotentiary

PLACE
"Hotel under the Star" in Paso Robles, California

TIME
The play is a story of the night of May 21-22, 1922

MUSIC
Music of Chopin and Paderewski

AUTHOR'S NOTES

- The play is based on true historical facts. It uses actual documents and quotes real statements. It is, however, a literary fiction.

- Events of Act 1 and the beginning of Act 2 occur simultaneously.
- Ignacy Paderewski is called in this play "The President", because this was his official title in Poland in 1919, "The President of the Council of Ministers". We have to explain that Poland at that time did not have the office of "The President". The Head of State was Józef Piłsudski who used the title of "The Leader" ("Naczelnik"), in reference to the title used by Tadeusz Kościuszko.

PROLOGUE

♪ In darkness we hear Paderewski's "Menuet à l'Antique." Ignacy Paderewski appears in a spotlight: He listens to the music. He puts his finger to his lips. The music fades off.

PADEREWSKI: It used to be... It's the past...

They were saying that music sings through his hands... That he is a piano charmer... Or, that under his touch the piano sounds like a whole symphonic orchestra... Indeed, he worked outÄand a work it was: hours, days, years of practicing—he worked out his own, unique, secret technique, known only to him. Nobody else could imitate it. Behold: when his right hand played one melody, and the left another, he was able, accelerating or slowing down—for a fraction of a second—the tempo of one or the other hand in order to play both melodies separately, and, at his will, to combine them, or to split them. This was his famous "Tempo rubato". This very secret provided his performance an incredible melodic richness, giving his listeners the impression that they were hearing the entire orchestra. Many proclaimed him a genius. The old Saint-Saëns, quibbled: "Paderewski is a genius who, additionally, plays piano." Both of them laughed. Paderewski was compared to the Shakespearian Prospero, who rules over the spirits and nature. Others wrote that, as Homeric Odysseus, he once navigates the turbulent Aegean sea waters, once a calm surface of the Ithaca harbor. Still others said that he plays as carried away by Promethean bursts of fire, here and there pierced by the Zeus' thunders... He was praised for combining intellectualism with sensualism, clashing the pianissimo whisper with Titanic power of his strokes... It was that way. No more.

A pause. Paderewski continues:

In the Spring of 1922 Ignacy Paderewski found himself in the small town of Paso Robles in California, located midway between San Francisco and Los Angeles, near two ranches he owned, Rancho San Ignatio and Rancho Santa Helena; both of them abundant with wine groves, and their soil expecting to be pregnant with oil. Paderewski stayed in the "Hotel under the Star." Actually, he rented the entire hotel.

Born in 1860, he wasÄat that timeÄsixty two years old. Behind him stretched long years of learning and growing as a pianist and composer; about a quarter of a century of a brilliant, successful carrier of a virtuoso, whose fame spread all over the world; several years of a political career as leader of Polish-Americans, and then as leader of all Poles—the President of the Council of Ministers of Poland. He resigned from music for politics, then, he was forced to resign from politics. He found himself as the crossroad.

All characters of the play appear one by one.

MISS WONDERWRITE I am Miss Wonderwrite, music critic. Master! The concert halls all over the world, are calling you, are inviting you. The realm of music is ready for the restoration of your reign. Critics, impresarios, followers, enthusiasts are anxiously waiting for your return.

PADEREWSKI But, after so many years of non-practice the pianist's fingers had lost their dexterity. Would it be possible to achieve full control of them again?

STRAKACZ: I am Sylvin Strakacz, personal secretary to the President Paderewski. Mister President, the office of the President of Poland is awaiting for you in Warsaw. You are the best candidate in the upcoming presidential election the most experienced, the most virtuous, the most worthy. Supporters, friends, admirers, and, indeed, crowds, call you back to Poland. Mister President, please, return to Poland and took the helm of the nation!

PADEREWSKI: But there were many other contenders for power in Poland. So many foes...

TROJANOWSKI: I am Stephen Trojanowski, Ignacy Paderewski's plenipotentiary. Rich Californian soil is promising you, sumptuous harvests of wine and offers you uncountable reserves of oil. Develop wineries! Drill for the black gold!

PADEREWSKI: But my artist's soul demurred on the very thought that instead of a pianist and composer I should become a wine grower and oil producer.

MISS GLORIA: I am Miss Gloria, owner of the "Hotel under the Star" in Paso Robles, Paderewski's home in California. The town of Paso Robles wants to keep you as its citizen, counting that your very name would attract tourists and business. We are offering you lucrative deals and tax brakes for your vineries, for your oil industry.

PADEREWSKI: I'm not yet ready to live the life of a pensionary cashing in only on my past.

FRONCZAK: I am doctor Fronczak of Buffalo, US Army colonel, personal physician and political advisor of Ignacy Paderewski. I suggest another option—to run for a political office in America, counting on the votes of the thousands of Polish-Americans.

PADEREWSKI: But to become a politician in America, rather than in Poland seems awkward to me...

HELENA: I am Helena Paderewska, yes, it's me. First a lover, than, the wife of the maestro. You haven't forget, my dear, I hope, our beautiful, quiet chateau in Riond Bosson, in Switzerland, as well as my hen farm there, my lovely hens...

PADEREWSKI: No, I haven't forget. That beautiful spot on the Geneva Lake shore was always a quiet harbor. Helena had her hen farm there. Her eccentric and costly hobby. Yet Riond Bosson demanded enormous sums of money for the upkeep. And there was no money in my coffers in 1922. I had given away my savings to the starving compatriots during the Great War, and spent them on running my office in Warsaw, refusing to accept the Presidential salary in Poland... In 1922, I, once a millionaire, had close to nothing...

MAYOR: I am the Mayor of the town of Ciężkowice in Poland. Mister Paderewski, we beg you, return to us. Not to the Warsaw Palace, but to your manor in Kąśna. We'll help you to start again. You'll help us to economically rise up the whole area. We'll built a spa, we'll attract people, we'll attract business...

PADEREWSKI: Yes. That was another option. To return to Poland. Not to Warsaw. But to the country. A country—loved, missed, longed for... To settle down in Kąśna, where I had an estate, to live a quiet life, to invite piano students, to culturally and economically upgrade the whole region... So, what? Music? Business? Politics? Heart? Duty? What this night should bring?

Blackout.

≡ ♪♪♪ ≡

ACT 1

The lobby of the "Hotel Paso Robles."

Miss Wonderwrite scribes in a notebook. Miss Gloria is busy at the counter. Strakacz brings two huge suitcases, an overcoat, and an umbrella. He returns a key to Miss Gloria.

STRAKACZ: Here's my key, Miss Gloria. The room is vacant. I shall probably never be back. Soon, the President's apartment will be empty too. In three-four weeks a telegram will come from Warsaw calling him to return...

MISS GLORIA: The postman brings all telegrams addressed to the hotel to me. And I will not give such a telegram to the President.

STRAKACZ: This would be a crime. There's no censorship of correspondence in America. You're joking.

MISS GLORIA: Of course, I'm joking. I'll take your telegram immediately to him and I personally run to the post office with a reply that he will not go. I know how I'm going to keep him here. I know, but I'll not tell you. You, Sylvin, you can return to that

Warsaw of yours. Have a nice trip. Or rather, have good weather on the Atlantic.

STRAKACZ: Thank you, Miss Gloria. I will have good weather and the President will have good weather too. He'll cross the Atlantic before the Autumn storms arrive.

MISS GLORIA: To run across the political storms in Poland! He'll go nowhere. He's well off here.

STRAKACZ: The President never chooses what is "well" for him. He is guided by the common good. I have to say goodbye to him. Who is going to replace me as his personal secretary?

MISS GLORIA: I will. I will replace you. Don't worry.

STRAKACZ: Precisely this very perspective worries me the most. Is there anybody to see him?

MISS GLORIA: Miss Wonderwrite, the famous journalist. She has been waiting since noon. *She smiles at Miss Wonderwrite, who returns the smile. Miss Gloria lowers her voice*: You know, that crazy bitch, who is following the President everywhere... In love with him... Like all these "Paddymaniacs," you know, all of them are crazy about Paderewski...

STRAKACZ: Are you not a Paddymaniac yourself?

MISS GLORIA: I'm a business woman. Investments, dividends, losses, gains. But if there were a profit in sight I would be ready to contract Paddymania.

STRAKACZ: I'm afraid that you see such profit on the horizon. The more I'm worry about the President.

MISS GLORIA: I'll take care of him. I'll prevent all the intruders from wasting his time. Especially that one...

STRAKACZ: The President might like to talk to Miss Wonderwrite. He highly values her writing. He gave her several interviews...

MISS GLORIA: Let her wait and rot. Besides, Mr. Trojanowski came first. There's also doctor Fronczak. He went for a walk. The President wants to see him tonight.

STRAKACZ: Yes, I know. The President wants to see him last, to have unlimited time for him. You, Miss Gloria, you should scrupulously screen all visitors—who, why, what for? Only letting in those who the President would decide to receive.

Not who came first, but whom the President wants to see first.

MISS GLORIA: That woman might sit here until midnight. I also have an urgent matter to discuss with the President.

STRAKACZ: Personal? Never disturb him with any personal affairs, please.

MISS GLORIA: It's not personal. It's public. The town's business. I suppose, you know that I'm a member of the Paso Robles Town Council.

STRAKACZ: Of course, I know. But I don't know if you know how to segregate personal from public affairs. Remember that public matters are always first with the President.

He addresses Miss Wonderwrite:

Hello, Miss Wonderwrite. My name is Strakacz, Sylvin Strakacz, President Paderewski's personal secretary. How nice to meet you. How do you do? How was your trip from New York? What's new in the grand world of music?

MISS WONDERWRITE: So, this is Mr. Strakacz? I finally get to meet you. I've heard so much about you. So, you are this famous, invisible master of ceremonies, who pulls all the strings and hides himself in the shadows? The indispensable personal secretary of the Maestro? What a handsome young man. I'd love to have in interview with you. Are you leaving?

STRAKACZ: I don't give interviews. Ever. That's up to the President. Yes, I'm leaving. There are pressing matters in Warsaw. The President has ordered me to go. I'm on my way to say goodby to him now. Would you excuse me...

MISS WONDERWRITE: What is the purpose of your trip?

STRAKACZ: It's a delicate mission...

MISS WONDERWRITE: A secret mission? You're an emissary?

I know that from Poland's crazy history. The emissary from the oppressed country sneaks out through the borders to travel to the free world. An emissary from abroad creeps into the country under the foreign rule. Are there still such conspiracies going on in Poland? Like during the times of the partitions?

STRAKACZ: Now it's not conspiracy but diplomacy. In a free and independent country. Excuse me, please. The President is waiting for me...

MISS WONDERWRITE: Please, tell him that I'm here. *To Miss Gloria*: I will not leave without seeing him. *To Strakacz*: I have some very important documents for him.

STRAKACZ: Documents? Perhaps I can deliver them?

MISS WONDERWRITE: Oh, no. I must do it personally. From my hand to his. I'll wait.

STRAKACZ: As you wish.

Strakacz is about to exit. At the same time the Mayor enters. He carries a valise and a bag. Strakacz looks at him and leaves. The Mayor goes to the counter.

MAYOR: Zimmer... Bitte...

MISS GLORIA: Are you German?

MAYOR: No, Polish.

MISS GLORIA: Don't you speak English?

MAYOR: Niks. Deutch sprechen. We were under Austrian rule. English a little bit. Albo po polsku.

MISS GLORIA: Polish? Fine. We all speak Polish here. The entire hotel is rented by the President.

MAYOR: President?

MISS GLORIA: President.

MAYOR: Paderewski?

MISS GLORIA: Paderewski.

MAYOR: Ignacy?

MISS GLORIA: Ignacy.

MAYOR: Znalazłem go!

MISS GLORIA: What did you say?

MAYOR: It was in Polish. I'll try English. But don't laugh at me.

MISS GLORIA: I won't. So, what did you say?

MAYOR: I found him! My uncle, living in Los Angeles writing me Paderewski staying in Paso Robles. I coming to see him all the way from Poland. Paderewski.

MISS GLORIA: To see Paderewski? Did you write with a request for an audience?

MAYOR: No...

MISS GLORIA Did you send a telegraph?

MAYOR No...

MISS GLORIA Did you phone to reserve a room?

MAYOR: No...

MISS GLORIA: So, you have to look for another hotel. We're booked. And you're not to get an audience with the President any time soon. He's extremely busy. There are many people waiting in line.

MAYOR: But I come, or rather I swim, from far away. From Europe. From Poland. From Kąśna.

MISS GLORIA: From where?

MAYOR: From Kąśna.

MISS GLORI:A Koushna? Never heard of it.

MAYOR: Kąśna. Or, Ciężkowice, rather. Would you, please, only tell him that the honorable Mayor of the town of Ciężkowice has arrived. The town of Ciężkowice. Near the city of Tarnów. With a delegation, that is, with a deputation, that is, with a plea... He'll know where I am from. He'll take me right away.

MISS GLORIA: First, I have to "take you..." Or not to take you... I own this hotel.

MAYOR: My dear lady, my fair lady, I beg you, might you have a free room for me?

MISS GLORIA: A free room? No.

MAYOR: That is, an empty room, an available room? I will pay you, of course. A small room? Very small?

MISS GLORIA: All right. Perhaps, I'll find a room for you. But as far as the audience with the President is concerned, you have to talk to me first and explain who, why, and what for. That is, who are you, why do you want to see the President, and what is your purpose. I'm now the President's personal secretary. I'll submit your case to him. Or, I'll not submit it. And only if I submit it, then, and only then, the President will decide whether to see you, or not.

MAYOR: What? First, I had to take a carriage from Ciężkowice to Tarnów, then I traveled three days and three nights by train from Tarnów to Bremen. Then, nine days by ship on the water to New York. Again three days by train to Los Angeles. I did not stay long with my uncle, only to drink a flask. And still one whole day to rich here. Almost two weeks. I even skipped Sunday Holy Mass. And you say "I'll submit" or "I'll not submit." It's almost like Austrian bureaucracy. Travel is expensive, even if the town is paying. I thought America was a free country and anybody could talk to anybody at their own will.

MISS GLORIA: Why so much noise? Why such nerves? It is precisely that freedom that allows us to meet whomever we like, and not to meet those whom we don't like. No Austrian Emperor is going to order us around.

MAYOR: So, I have to go? Two weeks again? For nothing? Well, that's fine. I'll return to Ciękowice and tell everybody. I'll even write a letter to a newspaper in Kraków, about how I was treated in America! What a viper secretary President Paderewski has! What is this famous American democracy!

MISS GLORIA: Poland would be better off learning the American democracy!

MAYOR: The old Polish saying has it "Thin or fat anybody can be an aristocrat." A mayor is no worse than a president.

MISS GLORIA: All right, all right. We'll talk about democracy later. About America too.

MAYOR: I not coming to argue about America. I coming to speak with the President about Poland. I want to humbly submit to the President our sincere request that he returns to Kąśna. The Ciężkowice Town Council and the whole population asked me to ask the President to coming back. He may now building a spa in Kąśna, as he wanted years ago. Yes, a spa, a new bridge, the ponds need fish, the stables horses...

MISS GLORIA: Not so fast. You'll submit all that to the President. Now, I give you the key. You'll unpack, change, shave... And then come down. I'll see what I can do for you. Maybe the President will even see you tonight?

MISS WONDERWRITE: I'll go first! I've been waiting since noon!

MISS GLORIA: The President will decide who goes first. Mr. Mayor, sir, here's your key. Room number four. Upstairs left.

She gives the key to the Mayor who leaves.

MISS WONDERWRITE: What is Mr. Strakacz doing there for so long? He's going to miss his train.

Dr. Fronczak enters and passes the lobby. Miss Wonderwrite stops him.

MISS WONDERWRITE: Doctor Fronczak? We met in Buffalo, in 1917, I believe.

FRONCZAK: And you are? Oh, yes, you are the famous music critic who, as the maestro once told me, understands his music best... Miss...

MISS WONDERWRITE: Miss Wonderwrite. That's me. Did the master indeed say that?

FRONCZAK: Yes. He thinks very highly of you.

MISS WONDERWRITE: I'm thrilled. He is the best pianist in the world. But he doesn't perform any more. Doctor, would you like to help me convince him to return to the piano? Without playing he'll wither, he'll fall ill...

FRONCZAK: I know. But, can he find enough strength to submit himself to the regimen of practicing twelve or more hours per day, as he did when he was at his zenith?

MISS WONDERWRITE: I'm sure, he will. I have an offer which might tip the scale. *She looks around and whispers in his ear.* How's that?

FRONCZAK: I have another offer for him, I can tell you. It'll be for him to choose. It's late and he probably wont see me tonight. I'll go to bed. Would you excuse me?

MISS WONDERWRITE: I will wait. And Euterpe too.

FRONCZAK: The muse of music?

MISS WONDERWRITE: You're a learned man, doctor. Euterpe longs to be embraced by him, again. I only want see his visage.

FRONCZAK; Good lack to both of you. Your and Euterpe.

Exits.

MISS WONDERWRITE: Charming gentleman.

Trojanowski stands up.

TROJANOWSKI: The President wanted to see me urgently. I'll go next.

MISS WONDERWRITE: I'll not allow this! You certainly have some economic business. I need to talk to him about art. The President always chooses art over anything materialistic.

MISS GLORIA: The President is now talking with Mr. Strakacz. Last meeting before the campaign. Both of you have to wait.

MISS WONDERWRITE: What campaign?

MISS GLORIA: You don't know? Mr. Strakacz is going to Warsaw to inaugurate the Paderewski's electoral campaign for Poland's presidency.

MISS WONDERWRITE: Mr. Strakacz did not tell me...

MISS GLORIA: He didn't tell you... But don't worry. We send Strakacz to the old country to get rid of him. Paderewski stays with us. Here. In America. We'll not allow him to go. We need him here.

MISS WONDERWRITE: Here? In this Californian god-forsaken hole? He'll stay in America! But not here. He'll stay in concert halls of the greatest cities.

MISS GLORIA: Everybody knows that he hasn't given concerts for years. How many? Seven, eight years?

MISS WONDERWRITE: He did not give solo recitals for seven years, four month, and—*she checks a notebook*—fourteen days, yes, fourteen. But he played either at political rallies or for small circles of the dearest friends, at the White House too. I heard him so many times...

MISS GLORIA: He's abandoned even that since his departure to Europe in 1918. He's been mute for more then three and half years. Correct? He returned to America more then a year ago, yet, he did not return to concert halls. Why? You don't know that either? The walls have ears. I've heard it many times. He sits at the piano, he starts playing, and immediately he blunders. That's why. Not the same fingers. He's not going to be a pianist anymore. Forget about a Paderewski virtuoso. There's no fuel for your Paddymania. He belongs to us now.

MISS WONDERWRITE: Are you his owner? You? He still has a wife, Madame Helena.

MISS GLORIA: Not I. Not I. We. The whole of Paso Robles population. We are his family now. He'll stay with us. You'll see. Besides, we have means to keep him here.

TROJANOWSKI: I don't know what means you are talking about, Miss Gloria, but I know what I'm holding for the President. Wine grows around. Crude oil bubbles under the soil. "Paderewski Zinfandel" will conquer the market, thanks to both its name and its taste. Oil doesn't even need a name. It's a dark gold.

MISS WONDERWRITE: He'll not stay here. I know him. He'll brake from the cage. He'll fly. As in old times. On music's wings... He... The modern immortal...

MISS GLORIA: Journalistic poetry. Cheap. We are preparing something real for him. With a dollar value on it. He's always liked to earn big money.

MISS WONDERWRITE: Money has never been his objective. Ever! If he earned it, he immediately gave away.

MISS GLORIA: Right. He gave away everything. Now, he'll need to accumulate again. We'll help him. We'll allow him to earn. Am I right, Mr. Trojanowski?

TROJANOWSKI: I concur. That's the deal.

MISS WONDERWRITE: The deal! The earnings! The money! It's all below the artist.

TROJANOWSKI: He is such an artist who knows how to count money. I was his impresario, before I became his plenipotentiary. I organized Maestro's concerts in Buffalo. Ten of them. Before of that I was in the oil industry.

MISS WONDERWRITE; Buffalo? I was there. I was there every time. I remember that famous concert in 1917, after which the Maestro called upon the Polish Americans to enlist to the Kościuszko Army.

TROJANOWSKI: Many responded...

MISS WONDERWRITE: Yes, yes, I remember. Big posters with only PADEREWSKI on them. And only the place and the hour.

TROJANOWSKI: It was my idea. PADEREWSKI. Enough!

MISS WONDERWRITE: The biggest room in the City Hall cramped. Poles. Americans. Workers from the steel mill, priests, military, old, young.

TROJANOWSKI: Yes, many young...

MISS WONDERWRITE: Entusiasm! Enters Maestro. Deafning ovation. Maestro sits at the piano. Deep silence. The Maestro performs Chopin. Outbreakes of cry. It was... It was as Chopins filled Paderewski's hands with love to Poland and Paderewski was giving this love to all listeners. This great, boundless, sacrificial, mistycal love... And after the concert, after the endless ovations the Maestro gave a speech about the predicament of

Poland, her sufferings under three cruel partitioners, and he said that Poland must be resurrected, that America must support that, and that all Polish-Americans must give their hearts, their money, and, if needed, their blood…

TROJANOWSKI: They gave blood…

MISS WONDERWRITE: That recruitment points to the voluntary Polish army in America are open—he annouced…

TROJANOWSKI; The first point was in Buffalo. A long line formed just after the concert…

MISS WONDERWRITE: Entusiasm. Chanting his name…

TROJANOWSKI: I know. I was there. And my son too. He went to that line…

MISS GLORIA: Did he enlist?

MISS WONDERWRITE: He did. I organized Maestro's meetings later on too.

MISS GLORIA: Meetings?

TROJANOWSKI: He gave speeches. He performed too. Every time he had to have his Steinway. A delicate task is was to move such a heavy piece from the train station to a hall. Half a day of tuning. He always checked himself.

MISS WONDERWRITE: So, you are my soulmate! You understand me. Help me, please, to convince the Maestro to return to music.

TROJANOWSKI: I will not. It would be too much for him now. He suffered enough at the keyboeard.

MISS WONDERWRITE: He was happy at the keyboard.

TROJANOWSKI: He was paying a too great price.

Enters Strakacz.

MISS GLORIA: He's not an artist anymore. He's a former artist.

TROJANOWSKI: And, alas, a former politician too.

MISS GLORIA: He's beginning to understand that.

MISS WONDERWRITE: You have no right to speak like this about him! I forbid you!

STRAKACZ: Some emotions? Quiet, please. These walls are paper thin, Miss Gloria. Every word is heard upstairs.

MISS GLORIA: It's the best hotel in California. Only you don't like it.

STRAKACZ: I doesn't matter to me. What matters is calm and good working conditions for the President. I'm leaving, anyway. The President will see Mr. Trojanowski now.

MISS WONDERWRITE: And what about me? Did you tell him that I'm waiting?

STRAKACZ: Yes. The President is very grateful to you, Miss Wonderwrite, for your visit and he will try very hard to find some time for you. But before this would be possible, he must look into some economic matters and take care of business. Mr. Trojanowski, the President is waiting for you.

TROJANOWSKI: I go... I go... *Exists.*

STRAKACZ: Did the automobile come for me?

MISS GLORIA: No, not yet. *To Miss Wonderwrite* Didn't I tell you? Economy, business, money—this is what preoccupies the President now. Not music.

MISS WONDERWRITE: So, I have to wait? I am ready for any sacrifice.

Enters Mayor—refreshed, changed.

MAYOR: *To Miss Gloria* How are things going? May I see the President?

MISS GLORIA: Not now. You have to wait. This lady is waiting too. And there are other visitors.

MAYOR: All right. I'll wait.

STRAKACZ: *To Miss Gloria* Who's this?

MISS GLORIA He came to see the President. He introduced himself as the Mayor of the town Tchenshkovitze, near the city of

Tarnoof in Europe. Have you heard about Tarnoof?

STRAKACZ: I have. It's a famous city. In Poland. *To Mayor*: I'm happy to welcome the Mayor of Ciężkowice. I'm Sylvin Strakacz, personal secretary to President Paderewski. How can I help you?

MAYOR: That lady said that she is the secretary.

MISS GLORIA: Because Mr. Strakacz is leaving. I'll substitute for him.

STRAKACZ: I haven't left yet. So, you came to see President Paderewski?

MAYOR: Yes, sir. I told that lady. I coming to beg President Paderewski to return to Kąśna. The Ciężkowice Town Council sending me and paying for the travel.

Kąśna belongs to Ciężkowice, you know. All the people asking me to go. All saying—tell Mr. Paderewski to return. He had a manor there, forests, fields, ponds. The ponds need fish. The stables horses. The people investments. Present owner of the estate is ready to sell it back. The town is ready to sell as much of the land as Mr. Paderewski would wish to buy for construction, for parks, for roads. Here's the Councils resolution. Years ago the Town Council did not want to sell him the grounds for building a spa, because, they said, people from abroad would come, walking around they would trample our pastures, they would be parading around undressed, what would they do in the bushes, who knows? Morality of the community would deteriorate. So, the Council opposed selling him more ground. He got angry and sold everything. We got nothing. Now we have a new Town Council. Now we understand progress. A huge progress is rolling through the world, as a snowball. Huge, fast progress. And we were left behind. So, we decided to ask Mr. Paderewski for pardon, to beg him for return, to bring money, to bring investments, to bring progress. I have all the documents. I have poems written by school students beseeching Mr. Paderewski... Here...

Strakacz interrupts him gently.

STRAKACZ: I understand. I understand, Mr. Mayor. It's a beautiful plan and a very interesting proposal. You have to present it to the

President. He might consider it. If he would return to the country, that is to Warsaw... not to Kąśna... he might want to offer his patronage to the program of Kąśna's development, reconstruction... progress... as you said. It is an option. It could have a certain symbolism. It could have political clout. Yes. You have to talk to the President.

♪ *An automobile horn is heard.*

It's for me. *He quickly exits and immediately returns.* Yes. It's my taxi. But I'll go inform the President that you're here, Mr. Mayor...

MISS GLORIA: I'll go. You'll be late for your train to Los Angeles.

STRAKACZ: It's an important political matter. I'll be back.

MISS GLORIA: You don't trust me?

STRAKACZ: All right. As soon, as Mr. Trojanowski returns, please, go to the President, introduce him to the Mayor's offer, and suggest that he sees him. I recommend him. Do you understand? I gave my permission for this meeting.

MISS GLORIA: I understand. And when the next clients come to see the President, I will cable you in Warsaw with a question of whether you recommend them or not.

STRAKACZ: Miss Gloria, please, don't joke about such serious matters. Please, consider your duties as the President's secretary with utter solemnity. I'll settle this last matter personally. *Exits.*

MISS GLORIA: *Shouts after him* You don't trust your closest collaborators! *To Mayor* He's right. He'll get you an audience right away, while I would think twice before I'd let you see the President.

MAYOR: A sharp gun. As a governor or a senator. Frightening.

MISS GLORIA: You're not sharp? With your Town Council?

MAYOR: It's different at home. The whole community backs me.

MISS GLORIA: And he is backed by the President.

MAYOR: President Paderewski, you mean? So, I am supposed to see him?

MISS GLORIA: This is what you came for. Isn't it?

MAYOR: I'm scared.

Returns Strakacz with Trojanowski.

STRAKACZ: The President will see you now, Mr. Mayor.

MAYOR: Me?

STRAKACZ: Right away.

MAYOR: Must I go?

STRAKACZ: He'll listen to you. Please, speak clearly and concisely. You brought some documents with you, yes? Show them and explain. You address the President, "Mister President." Good luck. I hope to see you in Poland soon. I'll cable you from Warsaw.

If you receive such a telegram, you must prepare yourself for a state visit: Men on horseback at the city gates, school children on the town main square with flowers, firemen orchestra, church choir singing "Gaude Mater Polonia," welcome speeches, not too long, but at least three the pastor, the mayor, the school-master. A reception in the best restaurant. Official talks in the Town Hall.

MAYOR: A state visit?

STRAKACZ: The President would came as the President of Poland. Now, you go to invite him. Upstairs!

MAYOR: Upstairs? The President of Poland?

STRAKACZ: Don't blow this opportunity. Good by. *He greets all present.* Mister Mayor. Mister Plenipotentiary. Miss Wonderwrite. Miss Gloria. I'm counting on you, Miss Gloria! Check the correspondence carefully. Most of all the telegrams from Warsaw. Good by.

He exists with his suitcases.

MISS GLORIA: A perfect secretary. A martinet, yet a good man. He'd go through fire and water for the President. But he's gone. Now we are at the helm. Go. The President is waiting.

MAYOR: I have to go?

MISS GLORIA: You asked for it.

MAYOR: Yes. But now I'm scared. Directly to the President? How about tomorrow?

MISS GLORIA: No. Now. It's his order.

MAYOR: Saint Michael, guard me!

MISS GLORIA: Don't lag. He might change his mind. This way!

MAYOR: This way? *He exits.*

MISS GLORIA: Bumpkin! I hope the President doesn't listen to his offers.

TROJANOWSKI: The President's in a very bad mood. Something is eating at him. He's weighing some heavy decisions.

MISS GLORIA: How did you do with him?

TROJANOWSKI: The reports from the wineries and the oil wells are good. He was pleased, but it didn't cheer him up. He ordered three new wells. But he doesn't want to visit them. You can feel oil under your feet, Miss Gloria. I remember once, in Texas, I got up early and went straight to the wells. We had a whole forest of them there. Gorgeous. The sun's orange flame is rising behind their tusswork making them dance in the air. I'm waking their direction. Suddenly, I feel that I have to turn and go back. Not to the rising sun, but the other way. West. The heat is mounting on my neck. I go a long way. And, it's like a chill. Something stops me. I know that this is the spot. When we drilled there, a black fountain gushed as high as I've ever seen. I'll find it here.

Helena Paderewska enters. She carries a box.

HELENA: Miss Gloria, how do you feed such birds? I found him on the balcony. He has a broken wing. He's all red. Look. Don't let him go.

MISS GLORIA: It's a Cardinal.

HELENA: Cardinal? What a name? It's somehow disrespectful. The Holy Church's prince?

MISS GLORIA: Cardinal. That's the name. You can find them all over America. Especially on the East Coast. Southern California too. Cardinal. The name surely comes from this red. Broken wing?

HELENA: He was grappling all over the balcony, but couldn't fly. I tossed a scarf on him and caught him. Then into a box. We have to bind his wing, immobilize it. What does such a Cardinal eat?

MISS GLORIA: Grains. From the bushes. There's plenty in front of the hotel.

TROJANOWSKI: Water too. Give him some water.

MISS GLORIA: I'll fetch a glass. Madame Helena, please, sit down. I'll be right back.

Helena sits down.

HELENA: Poor little one. Without me he would die. *She looks around.* Is this Miss Wonderwrite?

MISS WONDERWRITE: Yes, madame, its me. So good to see you.

HELENA: What are you doing here so late?

MISS WONDERWRITE: I simply wait. But I don't count time waiting for the Maestro.

HELENA: He won't see you, Miss. Why? He's no longer performing. You have nothing to write. We're about to leave for Switzerland. Escape from the journalists. My hens are waiting.

MISS WONDERWRITE: There's no escape from music lovers.

Miss Gloria returns with a glass of water. Helena takes it and unintentionally drinks.

HELENA: Thank you, Miss Gloria. And you, Miss Wonderwrite, what did you say? No escape from music lovers? Lovers? Why are you thrusting yourself on him all the time? Why do you pursue him from place to place? I tolerated it when he gave concerts. I tolerated it, because it helped his career. Somebody had to inform the public what a great pianist he was. But now? Enough. You have to go now. I'll tell him not to see you. Good night.

MISS WONDERWRITEL I also wrote about your great philanthropic deeds, madame Helena. You were so kind, so warm, so compassionate... You were a mother for all those young boys of the Kościuszko Army, for the orphans in Poland, for the hungry... I've always admired you! I worshiped you!

HELENA: Did you? Indeed?

MISS WONDERWRITE: You're a wonderful woman, madame Helena. You're brave. You're tender. Now you take care of this bird. The Cardinal. What a heart!

HELENA: My heart?

MISS WONDERWRITE: A most gentle heart! I wrote about your heart. And how good looking you were in that uniform of the "Polish White Cross" nurses' unit. A silver eagle on your chest and on the chest of the eagle a white cross. What a profound symbolism.

HELENA: Your wrote about me? You're so kind...

MISS WONDERWRITE: Entire stories, columns, news...

HELENA: There's nothing to write about anymore. The war is over. The wounded left hospitals. The dead stayed in the graveyards. America does not need us. Poland does not want us. So, Switzerland. We'll be leaving soon for Riond Bosson.

MISS WONDERWRITE: I'd like to present to the Maestro some offers, though. They are tempting. Perhaps the Maestro will consider...

HELENA: He has nothing to consider. I want Switzerland. You're getting on my nerves. Miss Gloria, please, call somebody to take her away. Arrest her! Do not allow her to see my husband. Prohibited. Get out! Get out! I hate you. *She smashes the box.* You've stolen my husband, all of you. I cant stand it! I cant look at you. Get her out of my sight. No. I shall go. A journalist. A Paddymaniac.

MISS WONDERWRITE: Madame Helena, calm down, please... You crushed the box...

A pause. Helena looks into the box.

HELENA: The bird. He is not moving.

She exits crying. A pause. The Mayor appears.

MAYOR: We had a good talk. He took the documents. He ordered me to stay for the night. He'll see me again tomorrow. That's nice. Kąśna will rejoice. Ciężkowice will grow.

♪ *A telephone rings at the reception desk.*

MISS GLORIA: Yes sir, yes, mister President. Right now? With cream? As usual. I'll send it right away in a hurry. *She puts down the receiver.* The President's ordered his evening coffee. It means a long night. *Exits.*

TROJANOWSKI: *To Miss Wonderwrite*: Maybe he'll call you now. Or the colonel.

MISS WONDERWRITE: Colonel Fronczak?

TROJANOWSKI: He has arrived this morning, summoned from Buffalo. The President greeted him warmly and asked him to wait. He might see him again tonight.

MISS WONDERWRITE: I know. That charming doctor-politician.

TROJANOWSKI: The same. Personal physician and personal political adviser. They both must be planning some new political action.

MISS WONDERWRITE: Politics again? I thought that the Maestro had enough of politics. He is an artist.

TROJANOWSKI: Now he is an industrialist. But who knows? He is obviously struggling with something. Or, God forbid, he is ill and that was the reason to have doctor Fronczak coming? I don't know. *To Mayor*: You, Mr. Mayor, have some rest. Two weeks journey. You deserve it. I'll go to bed too.

MAYOR: I'm not sleepy. I'll have a walk before I go to bed.

TROJANOWSKI: Only be careful. The streets are not well lit. Good night. *Exits.*

MAYOR: Does the President always stay so late?

MISS WONDERWRITE: Always. But in the old days he played the piano nightly. Now he gives audiences to people. He ponders over...

♪ *She interrupts, because the piano is heard from behind the scenes. We hear the beginning of Paderewski's "Variations and Fuga in E flat minor, Op 23", but soon after the beginning, the pianist errs. After a while, he resumes, this time slower, obviously too slow, he plays longer, but errs and interrupts again. He starts for the third time, he makes an error again, for a while he struggles, and gives up.*

MISS WONDERWRITE: Did you hear that?

MAYOR: I did. Is't the Maestro playing the piano?

MISS WONDERWRITE: It's him. He struggles. He hasn't play for years. But he'll return. Thank you Apollo!

MAYOR: He'll return to Kąśna. I'm telling you. *Exits to the outside.*

♪ *The telephone rings. Miss Gloria runs in and answers.*

MISS GLORIA: I am sorry, mister President, the cook left for the night, the kitchen is closed, but I'm just boiling water for your coffee... I'm sorry... Yes, I'm listening. How can I help you? Colonel Fronczak? Of course, I'll connect you with his room. Thank you, mister President. The coffee will be ready any minute. I know. Doctor Fronczak doesn't drink coffee. I'll have a glass of water for him. *She places a call to Dr. Fronczak's.* Doctor Fronczak? Colonel? Yes, sir, It's me, Gloria. I'm sorry to wake you up but the President wants to see you now. You're welcome, sir. I'll ring him. *She makes another call.* Mr. President? It's Gloria. I've just called Dr. Fronczak. He was already sound asleep. But he is getting ready. He asked you to excuse him, this will take some time. Yes. I'll have the coffee for you soon. You're welcome, sir, Mr. President. *She exits.*

♪ *We hear again the beginning of Paderewski's "Variations and Fuga in E flat minor, Op 23" and—similar to the previous one— struggle of the pianist to play it right. Enters Miss Gloria with a tray: a pot of coffee, a cap, sugar, milk, glass of water, ect. Miss Gloy and Miss Wonderwrite listen. Music stops.*

MISS WONDERWRITE: He's playing again. He's playing. He's returning.

MISS GLORIA: No. He's only testing his fingers. And they do not work. Here's the coffee for him. Good beginning of my tenure as a personal secretary.

MISS WONDERWRITE: A very large tray. I'll help you. *She tries to grab the tray.*

MISS GLORIA: Don't touch it. You're going to smash my best china!

MISS WONDERWRITE: Yet, I'd like to serve the Maestro. Don't tug it! You'll spill the coffee.

MISS GLORIA: Let it go, you crazy graphomaniac!

MISS WONDERWRITE: I'm holding firm! You let it go! You, geek!

The Mayor returns. They do not notice him.

MISS GLORIA: Loose it up!

MISS WONDERWRITE: I wont!

MISS GLORIA: A damn Paddymaniac!

MISS WONDERWRITE: A secretary-voluntary!

MISS GLORIA: Stop this nonsense!

MISS WONDERWRITE: It's not nonsense for me!

They wrestle silently for a while.

MISS GLORIA: We'll go together then.

MISS WONDERWRITE: All right. Together.

MISS GLORIA: We'll see from whom the President would like to get coffee.

MISS WONDERWRITE: We'll see. Let him decide.

MISS GLORIA: Carefully.

MISS WONDERWRITE: Very carefully.

On her way Miss Wonderwrite grabs her bag. They exit.

MAYOR: Hysterical women. If I were Mister Paderewski I'd kicked both their butts. Or I'd take both to bed. They would reconcile. *Exits.*

The stage is empty for a while. Helena enters with the box.

HELENA: The Cardinal must have a proper burial. The prince of the birds. What will become this red? Only white. *She puts her shawl on the box.* What else? Candles. There should be candles somewhere in the hotel in case of a power outage.

She finds candles at the counter. She lites them and puts them at either side of the box.

Did I strangle him? I surly did not want to. I wanted to fix his wing, to feed him, to heal him.

A pause. I never had a son.

ACT 2

Paderewski's apartment in "Hotel under the Star."

Paderewski is sitting at the piano with the cover closed. He moves his fingers, as if playing.

PADEREWSKI: Dumb wood. Dumb fingers.

Knocking at the door.

PADEREWSKI: Come in, please.

Enters Strakacz.

STRAKACZ: Do I disturb, Mr. President?

PADEREWSKI: No. You never disturb me, Sylvin.

STRAKACZ: I came to say goodby.

PADEREWSKI: I bless you and your mission.

STRAKACZ: Thank you, Mr. President.

PADEREWSKI: As I said, act delicately and prudently.

STRAKACZ: I'll follow all your instructions verbatim.

PADEREWSKI: In Paris you'll meet Mr. Dmowski. I gave you a letter for him. Do you have it?

STRAKACZ: Of course, Mr. President.

PADEREWSKI: Don't add anything to it. Only listen to the reply. Telegraph me immediately. In Warsaw you pay the visits precisely in the prescribed order: His Eminence Archbishop Primate Edmund Dalbor, the Commander Piłsudski, Chairman Witos, Chairman Daszyński, General Józef Haller, General Władysław Sikorski, and the Prime Minister, professor Nowak. During each visit use my Memorandum, which you have. You can quote it. But don't leave it with anybody. Don't leave any written note. After every visit you'll telegraph me. I'll send you further instructions.

STRAKACZ: I remember your Memorandum word for word, Mr. President. You know that I have a photographic memory.

PADEREWSKI: I've always esteemed your talents.

STRAKACZ: "Paragraph One. The historic hour. Independent Poland must elect a president. Based on the Constitution of March 17th, 1921, parliamentary elections will be held on November 5th, 1922. On November 12th, 1922, the National Assembly, consisting of the Sentae and the Sejm, will gather to elect a president. It is our historic, patriotic, national, and indeed our sacred duty to make a right and honest deicsion for the good of the coutnry...."

Helena enters without knocking. She carries a box.

HELENA: Look, Ignacy, I found this bird on the balcony. All red. He must have a broken wing. O, Sylvin, you're here, look...

STRAKACZ: Poor little one. A peculiar bird. I've never seen such red plumes. We have to fix his wing, feed him, water him... I can take him downstairs to Miss Gloria. She will certainly help...

HELENA: How kind of you. I will take care of him myself. Ignacy, don't stay too long.

PADEREWSKI: All right, Helena, all right. I'll come to bed soon...

HELENA: Sylvin, are you leaving?

STRAKACZ: I go to Warsaw.

HELENA: Not to Riond Bosson?

PADEREWSKI: Sylvin will visit Riond Bosson too, for sure...

HELENA: Goodbye then. Give my love to my hens. Adieu. *She exits.*

PADEREWSKI: Let's return to my Memorandum.

STRAKACZ: "Paragraph Two. Major forces of the nation. In historical order I list first the National movement of Chairman Roman Dmowski, who produced the Polish National Committee, based in Paris, recognized by the Allies as the legitimate representation of Poland. Chairman Dmowski, and myself worked hard at the Peace Conference in Versailles for the just frontiers of the newly restored Poland. The American government supported Poland, while the imperial arrogance of the British, the international Masonry and the Jews conspired against us... Secondly, the Socialist movement, headed by Commander Józef Piłsudski..."

PADEREWSKI, *interrupting delicately:* You remember it perfectly...

STRAKACZ: I do. So, after quoting your Memorandum, I'll move to my own message. I want your approval of its contents. I will say that above all the mass movements, political parties, and various factions, there is a moral movement, which stands above politics, above party lines, above the regional divisions. That movement is lead and represented by you, Mr. President. You—I'm going to continue—only you, are both beloved by the masses in the country and respected by the world leaders, only you look for the common good. Your utter unselfishness and benevolence even led you to offer, indeed, distribute, your own fortune to your suffering compatriots...

PADEREWSKI: I forbid you to speak about this.

STRAKACZ: I'm sorry. I'll follow your orders. I'll continue: Ignacy Paderewski is a man of God's Providence for Poland. He is a statesman and a diplomat, he is a world renowned artist and a soul of the highest order...

PADEREWSKI: To much about me. You have to address first of all the needs of the country and the challenges Poland faces. My humble figure must be situated only within this context.

STRAKACZ: I'll return to the Memorandum then "Only the unity and solidarity of all who are in the nation the best, the wisest, the most altruistic, and the most generous might overcome current divisions and steer the country towards progress and prosperity. The President should be this unifying force..."

PADEREWSKI, *interrupting delicately again:* Thank you, Sylvin. I have full confidence in your wisdom and tact. Even more than in your memory. You are prepared. You can go.

STRAKACZ: I go with hope. I know from the telegraphs that the number of your supporters is growing. All the more, because the present—both political and economic—situation of the country is really bad. The government has lost confidence. The economy is drowning. Prices are sky rocketing. Corruption spreads. It's a perfect time for you to return to Poland, and to launch the presidential campaign promising to change all that. Which you will! Our people in Warsaw vow that if only you announce the date of your return they will immediately start to rally the public opinion on your side. Your election is certain. I see these crowds greeting you at the Warsaw railway station. They will be even bigger than in 1919, when you triumphantly returned from America...

PADEREWSKI: But won't I hear hostile whistling of Piłsudski's officers?

STRAKACZ: Piłsudski knows that you always have respected him and never opposed him. Why should he oppose you now?

PADEREWSKI: And the Daszyński's labor-unions? They know how to stage street demonstrations.

STRAKACZ: A demonstration might be confronted by a counter-demonstration. If only you permit me...

PADEREWSKI: I will not patronize street fights. I would return not to divide but to unify the nation. And what about the communists?

STRAKACZ: They unmasked themselves as the Bolsheviks agents during the war of 1920. They do not matter, although they are still dangerous.

PADEREWSKI: I sailed from England to Gdańsk through mines fields in 1918... The Germans shot at my hotel windows in Poznań... I'm not afraid.

STRAKACZ: Everybody knows your courage and your constancy.

PADEREWSKI: This might not be enough to win the majority.

STRAKACZ: I go to create that majority.

PADEREWSKI: Go. Travel safely. Act carefully. Inform me about your every move. And remember the final decision about declaring myself as a candidate for the Presidency belongs only to me.

STRAKACZ: Yes, Mr. President. I understand. Oh, Miss Wonderwrite, that music critic from New York is waiting downstairs. Would you like to see her?

PADEREWSKI: What for? I don't perform anymore. But we have to be courteous with women. Please, tell her that I would like to talk to her and I will do my best to have time for her. But first I must see Stefan Trojanowski.

STRAKACZ: I repeat that. Good bye Mr. President. I shall see you in Warsaw.

PADEREWSKI: Goodbye. Godspeed.

Strakacz exits.

Paderewski circles the piano. Knocking at the door.

PADEREWSKI: Come in.

Trojanowski enters.

TROJANOWSKI: You called me, Mr. President. Here I am.

PADEREWSKI: Yes. It's late. I'm sorry. Yet, I've decided to reach certain decisions tonight. So, let's talk business. Oh, wait a second... Did you receive any reply from Warsaw about that military pension... After you son...

TROJANOWSKI: I did.

PADEREWSKI: Tell me.

TROJANOWSKI: Refusal.

PADEREWSKI: Impossible.

TROJANOWSKI: Flat-out refusal. I have this document. *He pulls the document out.* They say that my son was an American citizen, so Poland is not obliged to pay me any retribution, any pension. I have to write to the US government, thy tell me.

PADEREWSKI: He was an American, but he volunteered for the Polish army, organized under the American auspices. He considered himself a Pole even if he was born in America and had American citizenship. He was a Polish soldier. He died in Poland. For Poland.

TROJANOWSKI: I wrote them that. Just as you told me. Word for word. I attached your supporting letter with your signature. They did not respect even you.

PADEREWSKI: I don't matter here. What matters is honesty and justice. What matters is that you're wronged at present, and the memory of your son is distorted for the whole future of Poland's history. What was his name? Stanislaus?

TROJANOWSKI: Stan. Stanislaus. From the first group of the volunteers from Buffalo. They spent the whole winter in the Niagara-on-the-Lake camp under the tents. At training they were so hot that snow melted when they crawled.

PADEREWSKI: I know. I visited them. Oh, how they marched in that parade. The Polish army. After a century of bondage! Polish soldiers once again! Infantry. In their blue uniforms, puttees on their legs, rifles with bayonets in hand... But I saw in them the galloping horseback the winged calvary...

TROJANOWSKI: On the battlefields they were no worse then the winged knights. First, in France. Then, in Poland. There he fell. On his motherland bosom.

PADEREWSKI: Don't cry for him. He gave his life for Poland. And Poland lives again.

TROJANOWSKI: I know, Mr. President. But it's hard to swallow. In Poland they took him for a foreigner. There's no justice there since you left.

PADEREWSKI: Listen. I promise. I solemnly promise you that if I return to Poland, I will find this pension for the American father of the Polish soldier even under ground. Perhaps, it's the most important reason for me to return. Yes. Definitely. I must return to the county and demand justice for your, for your son, for the ten thousand who fell. And for all those betrayed, humiliated, deceived...

TROJANOWSKI: Don't go anywhere, Mr. President. Forgive me, but they do not want you in Poland. It's different here. America respects you. You have land here. Your own land. Wine will give you fruit. Oil will burst under your feet. It's a munificent country.

PADEREWSKI: Is this your advice? Maybe you're right. Yet, Stan's case mustn't remain unsolved. How could I pay you back, all of you, who send your children to war, death, wounds, all of you who returned from the war disabled?

TROJANOWSKI: You hired me and gave me a living. You send help to others. People know that. You're our father.

PADEREWSKI: People know?

TROJANOWSKI: They do. Here, in America, you are among your own, your Polish flock. And the Americans are your own too. They will not harm you. You can settle down here.

PADEREWSKI: I love America. Yes. What a beautiful country. How free the people are. I came to love America because she is as she is, and because of Poland.

Do you know that during the times of captivity, America was the only country on the globe where Poles could live as free people, enjoying the same freedom as everybody else? For this freedom

Poles flocked to America. And America strengthened their faith that Poland might be a free country too. A free country again. Because of this belief your son volunteered for the Polish army in America.

TROJANOWSKI: Yes. He believed that. The fact that he was an American did not stop him from giving his life for Poland.

PADEREWSKI: So, there's no contradiction between being an American and loving Poland? Is that your advice for me?

TROJANOWSKI: Yes, Mr. President. You are yourself, which means you are a Pole. But in America you are at home. You are an American. There's no conflict. Look into the books and the reports from the wineries, form the oil fields. It's all yours. Your America.

They both look into the books opened by Trojanowski.

PADEREWSKI: Thirty barrels of red "Paderewski Zinfandel" to San Francisco. Thirty barrels of the red... to Los Angeles... Ten barrels of the red to San Louis Obispo port... French vessel... "Princess Margot" of Tulon... Isn't too bold—to ship Californian wine to France?

TROJANOWSKI: Red "Paderewski Zinfandel" will stand the competition.

PADEREWSKI: Even if it is good, the French would not admit it.

TROJANOWSKI: We're shipping it to the world wine fair in Aix-en-Provence, with an international jury. Blind wine tasting. Everybody will think that it's some new Provencal variety. And here surprise. California! "Paderewski Zinfandel!" I believe in gold medal. The French will be forced to buy these ten barrels, and order more!

PADEREWSKI: All right. And what about white "Zinfandel?"

TROJANOWSKI: I'm not shipping it to France. We're working day and night. But it must take time. In five years we'll be sure of it.

Maybe earlier. Please, taste. May I pour?

PADEREWSKI: Yes, please.

Trojanowski opens two bottles and pours wine to four glasses. They taste.

TROJANOWSKI: First, the red.

PADEREWSKI: No objections. We'll conquer France.

TROJANOWSKI: You are a connoisseur.

PADEREWSKI: Now, white.

TROJANOWSKI At your service...

PADEREWSKI: It is not a white. It is a sort of an amber. Or a Sequoia skin from Yellowstone...

TROJANOWSKI: Not a Sequoia, rather a gold, a genuine, dark, Californian gold.

PADEREWSKI: Too sweet.

TROJANOWSKI: You're right. But we'll get there. And when we finally balance it right it will be unique. Neither France nor Italy would have such. This is going to be our gold streak. To your health. To our liquid gold.

PADEREWSKI: Liquid gold? So, what about oil?

TROJANOWSKI: It'll explode! Neighboring wells are already pumping like crazy. We'll strike it too. It's a matter of days. Come with me for a walk in the fields. You'll find it yourself.

PADEREWSKI: I prefer walking the wine groves.

TROJANOWSKI: Nevertheless, I would suggest, we have to drill, let's say, five new wells.

PADEREWSKI: How much is one well?

TROJANOWSKI: About five thousand dollars.

PADEREWSKI: All right. Order two new wells. We have to be careful with money.

TROJANOWSKI: As you decide. But I guarantee that there's gold. Black gold.

PADEREWSKI: Are you sure?

TROJANOWSKI: It's waiting for you.

PADEREWSKI: Well... Invest in three wells then. Inform me about the progress.

TROJANOWSKI: Yes, Mr. President. Immediately. Gold...

Knocking at the door.

PADEREWSKI: Come in.

Strakacz enters.

STRAKACZ: Excuse me, Mr. President, it's me, once more... The Mayor of the town of Ciężkowice has just arrived. You remember, Ciężkowice near Kąśna in Poland?

PADEREWSKI: Kąśna? So many years... What does he want?

STRAKACZ: He wants to petition you to return to your former estate of Kąśna.

PADEREWSKI: What an idea! It's a forgotten affair. Impossible.

STRAKACZ: Yet, in a certain constellation, this might be politically advantageous. To own a land again in Poland, a country estate.

PADEREWSKI: I loved that place. The manor. The forests...

STRAKACZ: Thus, it could also be emotionally beneficial. Please, consider receiving this Mayor. I would recommend it.

TROJANOWSKI: I would not. The President has his land here. And a profitable one. Kąśna was a well without a bottom—to only throw money in.

STRAKACZ: I understand Mr. Plenipotentiary's position, but on one side of the scale we have economy, certainly important, on the other side we have political profits and something so volatile as love of the country.

PADEREWSKI: I'll see him. Call him, please. And once more have a good journey.

STRAKACZ: Thank you, Mr. President.

TROJANOWSKI: I'll go too. I did report to you all facts and figures.

PADEREWSKI: Thank you, Stephen. Thank you, Silvin. God be with you.

Exit Strakacz and Trojanowski.

Paderewski sits at the piano. Knocking at the door. Paderewski stands up.

PADEREWSKI: Come in, please.

Mayor enters hesitantly.

PADEREWSKI: The Mayor of the town of Ciężkowice, am I right? My secretary has informed me. Welcome. Such a long way. How are you? How are things going in Kąśna? How are the Kordębskis?

MAYOR: They barley make ends meet. They want to sell the estate.

PADEREWSKI: To sell?

MAYOR: To you, Mr. President.

PADEREWSKI: Really? I'm not rich enough. Besides, I'm spoiled by the honest business practices in America, and I don't know how I would deal with Polish swindlers. Years ago, when I was buying Kąśna and running it, they robed me in broad daylight. No. I tried Kąsna once and I was nipped. There will be no encore.

MAYOR: Encore?

PADEREWSKI: Additional performance. It's a beautiful countryside. Kąśna... Ciężkowice... Forests... the manor... the fields... But as far as the economy of it was concerned, I remember only investments with no profit. I learned the hard way that I didn't have adequate money for the upkeep of that estate. Even my lucrative American piano tournées didn't bring enough.

MAYOR: Turnes?

PADEREWSKI: Travels. Travels and concerts all over America. I had to sell.

MAYOR: We know that something did not work that time. You were only spending money and you earned nothing. We know. It's all in the books. You restored the manor. New roof. Fireplaces. Plumbing. Bathrooms. Electricity. Even a telephone. A dam on the river and a dynamo. Brick factory. Mechanical diary. A quarry. You stocked the ponds with fish. You brought horses and cows.

You bought farming machinery. And the land reclamations, the gardens, stables, cowsheds, hen houses...

PADEREWSKI: Hen houses were the priority...

MAYOR: We know everything. We remember everything. We are grateful for everything. For the kindergarten, for the library, for the new bell on the church's tower. For those parties which you were throwing at the end of harvest. The whole countryside was attending. Those hams, those sausages, those sirloins, that vodka... We are grateful for all.

PADEREWSKI: A little late this gratitude comes...

MAYOR: Mea culpa! Nostra culpa! Our fault. But it was twenty years ago. Our grandfathers and fathers were ungrateful. We shall be thankful. We know that besides all the investments in the estate you wanted to build a spa. The Town Council would not allow that. But now we will. We will not only give you permission, but we beg you to do it. The Town Council of Ciężkowice asks you to build a spa, bring people. Let them sow money, we'll harvest it. And you, Mr. President, you will sit at the piano in the manor, only you thump the keys, go to the balcony, look at that whole progress, you return to the piano, strike a note, you drink coffee, you play bridge, you entertain guests, you enjoy yourself. The children of Kąśna also ask you to return. The memory is passed from generation to generation that, those twenty years ago, you once took all the children from the surrounding villages to a circus in Tarnów. So our children beseech you to return and take them to a circus...

PADEREWSKI: To a circus?

MAYOR: Yes. Thus, I came here to submit to you, Mr. President, that we want you to return. We humbly ask you. Here's the petition with all the signatures of the citizens. Here is the initial calculation of how much money you should bring, because money, of course, would be needed. For construction, bridges, roads, ponds, and the manor.

PADEREWSKI: Indeed, years ago I wanted to invest in Ciężkowice, to build a spa...

MAYOR: I know. But the Councilmen were stupid. They didn't understand what progress is rolling all over the world, how to do business. So, they opposed you. They didn't want the spa. They said that people from the big cities would come, they would walk everywhere, trample the pastures, dress indecently, and who knows what they would do in the bushes? Morality would deteriorate, hell's gates would open and devour all. But now we have a new Town Council. We understand what is new in the world, we want progress, development, growth, modernity, money. We implore you on our knees. *He kneels.* Please, return!

PADEREWSKI: Mr. Mayor. What are you doing! We're in America. Democracy! Get up!

MAYOR: I'll stay on my knees until you, Mr. President say that you shall return.

PADEREWSKI: I'll not say that. Not now. Enough of this. Sit down. I am very happy that I am well remembered in Kąśna...

MAYOR: And in Ciężkowice, in Tarnów, in Kraków, and everywhere around!

PADEREWSKI: Thank you. Thank you very much for you kindness. When you return home, tell everybody...

MAYOR: But will you return?

PADEREWSKI: It is not excluded. But a special constellation should shape for that... If I were to return to the country... That is to Warsaw... Perhaps, Kąśna could be my summer residence...

MAYOR: Deo Gratias! So, we can have hope?

PADEREWSKI: Only if so many various elements would fit together. They are beyond your control. Mine too. Kąśna... Tarnów... Kraków And what about the rest of the Galicia?

MAYOR: The whole country!

Helena enters without knocking.

HELENA: Good night, sir Mayor. Enough of this audience. We are not going to Kąśna. *To Paderewski* You, Ignacy, don't stay so late. To bed, to bed. Time to sleep. Other clients might tarry until tomorrow. I'm waiting. *To Mayor*: I said, good night.

MAYOR: I beg your pardon, Madame?

HELENA: Good night. *She exits.*

PADEREWSKI: Leave me these documents, Mayor. I'll examine them. We'll talk again tomorrow. Good night.

MAYOR: I humbly thank you, Mr. President. Most humbly.

♪ *Mayor exits. Paderewski lites two candles and puts them on the piano. He opens the cover of the keyboard. Places his fingers on the keys. He begins playing his "Variations and Fuga in E flat minor, Op 23", but soon after the beginning, he errs. After a while, he resumes, this time slower, obviously too slow, he plays longer, but errs and interrupts again. He starts for the third time, he makes an error again, he struggles for a while, and gives up.*

PADEREWSKI: My fingers don't work. The doors to the concert halls are shut. I have to send this chest back to its owner, Mr. Steinway. Instead of a piano, I should set a coffin here. Lay in it voluntarily. And not wait for a pianist resurrection. Who am I tonight? A statesman? A virtuoso? A businessman? A fugitive? I'm nobody. So, whom should I be? Tomorrow? In a year? Until the end of my days?

♪ *He—again—begins playing his "Variations and Fuga in E flat minor, Op 23", but soon after the beginning, he errs. He resumes, but errs and interrupts again. He starts for the third time, he makes an error again, for a while he struggles, and gives up.*

PADEREWSKI: No. I'm not a pianist anymore. But how should a virtuoso not performing any more? The tunes, the music, the silence of the audience and its ovations are for him the indispensable doses of oxygen. Without them he suffocates. And how to abandon the piano—a fierce enemy whom I have always conquered, the only true friend who never betrayed me, the only discrete confidant?

Knocking at the door. Paderewski stands up and goes to the balcony. He shouts from there:

Come in, please.

Enter Miss Gloria and Miss Wonderwrite carrying the tray with coffee.

MISS WONDERWRITE: You've ordered coffee, Maestro...

PADEREWSKI: At the reception desk.

MISS GLORIA: Yes. I receive your call. Here's some delicious coffee.

MISS WONDERWRITE: I wanted to help Miss Gloria, to bring it...

MISS GLORIA: Sylvin departed, so, I took over his duties. I made your coffee myself.

MISS WONDERWRITE: But I brought it.

MISS GLORIA: Not asked to do it.

PADEREWSKI: I thank you. I thank both of you. Please, put it down, somewhere. You're so kind.

MISS WONDERWRITE: Silvin's departure truly creates a need for a personal secretary for you, Maestro. I can substitute for him. You require a secretary who understands you and who understands art. I wrote about you, Maestro... I interviewed you so many times... I attended your every concert.

PADEREWSKI: There will be no concerts anymore.

MISS GLORIA: You just need a professional, business help, Mr. President. Sylvin appointed me your personal secretary. I would like to introduce you to some matters which demand your immediate attention...

MISS WONDERWRITE: There will be concerts, Maestro! I firmly believe in this. I had to come here and share this faith with you, Maestro. And, perhaps, to just pen down some of your new thoughts on art... on music...

MISS GLORIA: Don't interrupt!

MISS WONDERWRITE: I also brought some very interesting proposals from Mr. Steinway...

MISS GLORIA: Mr. Paderewski is not interested in any proposals from Steinway. As I was saying... There are some pressing matters.

I have the braking news from a session of the Paso Robles Town Council. We won! All my motions were accepted and passed by unanimous vote. I counted on the Republicans, but the Democrats, usually unsensitive to business, also understood that there are great things about to happen—investments, infrastructure, tourists inflow and, consequently, dollar influx. They voted "yea" too. Please, listen...

She looks into her notebook.

First, the Town Council voted to offer you significant tax brakes for twenty five years in case you increase investments in wine production. Let "Paderewski Zinfandel" flood California, America, France, the whole world. Wine groves, wineries, cellars... The same refers to oil production. Tax brakes for twenty five years. I see these never ending trains of vats with oil. We'll build a pipe-line to a see terminal...

MISS WONDERWRITE: Don't listen to her, maestro. It's not in your sphere. Let's talk about music. Your famous "tempo rubato." I was the first to understand how you use it. I was the first to write about it, based, of course, on an interview with you. Did you approve my interpretation, master?

PADEREWSKI: Yes. You had it right. "Tempo rubato..." Yes... I explained to you that this Italian term, "Tempo rubato," can't be translated literally, as a "stolen tempo," or "robbed tempo." Such a translation is not acceptable. Nobody steels anything from anybody. Nobody robs anybody. Yet, "Tempo rubato" means a certain disregard to generally accepted rules of the rhythm and the tempo. Chopin used to use "Tempo rubato" frequently as a performer. So did List.

MISS WONDERWRITE: And then you, master.

MISS GLORIA: Try my coffee, sir, please. Milk? Sugar? The usual? Returning to the business.

Number two: the town of Paso Robles, expecting your settling down here, wants to organize a world, yearly festival of music and wine. The town invites you to accept the role of the honorary president of such a festival and to invite well known virtuosos, critics, impresarios—your friends—from all over the world. Wine and oil producers should be invited too. For giving us permission to use your name for advertising the festival, we will pay you one hundred thousand dollars for each festival, every year, not bad, huh? In addition, you'll get a certain percentage of the profits from the festival. Depending on the attendance, from ten to twenty percent. The more guests and emptied bottles of wine, and cisterns of oil sold, the more for you. What do you think?

PADEREWSKI: What do I think? I have always thought that the "Tempo rubato" is a necessary means of expression of a virtuoso. The rhythm is the life of a musical work. A piece which I play must live its own life. What did you say, Miss Gloria?

MISS GLORIA: One hundred thousand dollars for your name for advertising the festival, and from ten to twenty percent from total gains.

PADEREWSKI: One hundred thousands...ten... twenty...

MISS WONDERWRITE: Back to "Tempo rubato!" Initially, you were criticized for its use. Even George Bernard Shaw wrote in 1890, after your concert in London, that your "Tempo rubato" bordered to a haphazard interpretation.

PADEREWSKI: I did not always agree with Mr. Shaw, although I consider him a good playwright. "Tempo rubato" was my, let's call it that way, because we are in America, well, "Tempo rubato" was my "Trade mark." Or my "specialité de la maison," as the French say.

MISS GLORIA: A "Trade Mark!" Fantastic! We can call our festival "Paderewski's Tempo Rubato in Paso Robles."

MISS WONDERWRITE: How trivial! How dare you! We are talking about art. Master, don't listen to her. Tell me, rather, why did you pay such an importance to your "Tempo rubato?"

PADEREWSKI: Because, only by using "Tempo rubato" was I able to give the works of different composers my own expression. "Tempo rubato" was a duality of the tempo of the right hand and of the left hand. A duality of a fraction of a fraction of a second. And it is I who rules over that fraction. Now, I even think that using "Tempo rubato" was indeed "steeling" those works from their composers. I became "owner" of those works. When I played them—they became my own. You see, there's a subtle, difficult to apprehend, yet, absolutely clear border between a piano player and a piano virtuoso. A performance might be excellent, but it remains an interpretation. The virtuosity is a creation.

MISS GLORIA: Returning to the festival "Paderewski's Tempo Rubato in Paso Robles..." Oh, I would forget... The Town Council decided to bestow on you the "Honorary Citizeship" of the Town of Paso Robles. We'll announce it when you decide...

MISS WONDERWRITE: Yes! Virtuosity is creation. The critics gradually comprehended that your "Tempo rubato" doesn't destroy the composition you play, but rather gives it a new, revealing iridescence.

MISS GLORIA: Number three. I already have a small concert hall in my hotel. The very day you agree to enter into a business partnership with the town—the town will start the construction of a new, large concert hall with two thousand seats and will pay for the whole project. If necessary, we'll build a whole philharmonic hall, and later, perhaps an opera. Money will come!

MISS WONDERWRITE: Money!

MISS GLORIA: So, what, Mr. Paderewski? You're not going to get such an offer anywhere in the world. Only in Paso Robles. Naturally, I will be appointed the general manager of the festival. You'll be the honorary president. Deal?

PADEREWSKI: It's truly a very generous offer.

MISS GLORIA: Profitable, first of all. Profitable!

PADEREWSKI: Profitable. I agree.

MISS GLORIA: We'll call a press conference tomorrow and announce the big news.

PADEREWSKI: I'd like to have some time to ponder on it...

MISS WONDERWRITE: Certainly! How can you be so pushy, Miss Gloria. How can you hasten the Maestro? Business. Percentages. Dollars. These are not the issues worthy of the Maestro's attention. Master, your entire past binds you to art!

MISS GLORIA: Don't look back, Paderewski. It's America. Here we only look forward.

PADEREWSKI: I've been admiring America and the Americans since my first visit.

MISS GLORIA: You're one of us. We have to combine our forces.

MISS WONDERWRITE: You're an artist. Souls' ruler. Don't listen to the call of money.

PADEREWSKI: You always were very kind to me, Miss Wonderwrite. I've valued your opinions about my music, my interpretations... But, indeed, this belongs to the past.

MISS GLORIA *to Miss Wonderwrite:* I told you. What counts is the future.

MISS WONDERWRITE: From that past, you, Master, you will throw a bridge to your future artistic triumphs. You have to return to your lyre, that is to the piano.

PADEREWSKI: It's out of the question.

MISS GLORIA: See!

MISS WONDERWRITE: Without you the music world is shadowy and pale. It's lacking something without which it can't live a life full and vital. There are many good pianist around, but there's only one Paderewski.

PADEREWSKI: I'm already a history. I am forgotten.

MISS WONDERWRITE: No! Here's the proof. She pulls out a poster from her bag. She hads it to Paderewski.

PADEREWSKI: What's this?

MISS WONDERWRITE: The Steinway Company sends a poster for your acceptance with a photograph of you—you, their most famous customer. See, Master, these two inscriptions: "Steinway the Instrument of the Immortals" and "Paderewski and His Steinway." The company wishes the Maestro good health and kindly asks when the Maestro might condescend to give a concert in New York. They propose November 1922. They will underwrite all the production costs. Signed Steinway and Sons, Steinway Hall, 109 East Fourteen Street, New York.

Paderewski takes the poster, examines it, and tears it into pieces which he throws on the floor.

MISS GLORIA: Bravo maestro! There's a real man of action.

MISS WONDERWRITE: Maestro... You shouldn't do this...

PADEREWSKI: I do not think about giving concerts anymore. It's a closed book.

MISS WONDERWRITE: No. These can't be words of a Master, the public's deity, the critics' favorite, the impresarios jewel. Your were celebrated, praised, worshipped, loved...

MISS GLORIA: You are unmasking yourself, Miss Wonderwrite. Hysterical Paddymaniac.

MISS WONDERWRITE: You've already unmasked yourself. Insensitive business woman.

PADEREWSKI: Miss Wonderwrite, I thank you for your encouragement. Miss Gloria, I'm grateful to you for opening these new horizons for me.

MISS GLORIA: My pleasure.

PADEREWSKI: But, I must tell both of you I am not ready. Neither for the piano, nor for the business.

MISS WONDERWRITE: Yet...

PADEREWSKI: Miss Wonderwrite, I've always been open with you. So, this time I'm also going to tell you the truth. My fingers are not fit. I haven't played for too long. Rather, I haven't practice. You know, perhaps only you know, that the virtuoso's practice—these six, eight, or sometimes twelve, or even seventeen hours per day—is a very hard labor. It's a slavery. It's an extortion of time and effort which a virtuoso imposes on himself. It happened sometimes, that I hadto work, yes, yes, for seventeen hours—with only one hour for eating and six for sleep. This necessity to constantly practice is a dark, even tragical side of the life of a musician-artist. Hidden from the public. But without it there's no success. Without it I would not begin a concert.

MISS WONDERWRITE: Yes, Master. I know. Perhaps I am the only one who understands...

PADEREWSKI: I haven't practiced that way in almost eight years. Every performance requires such an incredible amount of physical work and mental effort... I'll be flat honest with you, Miss Wonderwrite, and with you, Miss Gloria, too. I'm sixty two years old. I've got arthritis. The fourth finger of my left hand is still not fully sound, after I overworked it during my second American tour in 1893.

MISS WONDERWRITE: I know. I saw blood on the keyboard after your concert in Boston. After unending rounds of applause and encores, ah, I knew that each one was torture for you, when you walked off stage for the last time, I made my way through the throng, I climbed on the stage and collected blood from the keys with my handkerchief. Your blood... Then, following you step by step, from one city to another, from one concert to another, I repeated that twenty two more times... These handkerchiefs... I keep them in a special case... a reliquary...

PADEREWSKI: I am moved... I knew that my admirers were able watch for me for hours... Once, two of them attacked me in my dressing room and, in spite of my desperate resistance, cut of a tuft of my hair... But to collect my blood... Those concerts with a bleeding finger might be called a "heroic tour"Äborrowing the title from Beethoven, of course...

MISS WONDERWRITE: Your playing was always heroic. I heard pain in it. I knew that hurting your finger to the point of bleeding you suffered physically. But your music was expressing a metaphysical suffering of the human spirit struggling with the gravity of the matter. A fight you've always won. I heard in your playing a lament for your tormented country. You resurrected Poland. Now, you, yourself have to resurrect as a virtuoso.

PADEREWSKI: As a virtuoso? Not a composer?

MISS WONDERWRITE: As a composer too! The public awaits your new compositions, the conductors wait for them, the managers of the opera houses, the singers... I know, that having such a busy schedule as a virtuoso you were not able to compose enough. But now, after retiring from politics, and returning to the concert halls...

PADEREWSKI: I know nothing about that return.

MISS WONDERWRITE: ...after your triumphant return to the piano! As a virtuoso, you came after List and Rubinstein. You surpassed them. As a composer you came after Mozart and Chopin. You can surpass them too. You've composed masterpieces, but there's not enough of them. You've entered on the peaks, but you can create new heights, exploding your Titanic energy...

PADEREWSKI: Too much enthusiasm...

MISS GLORIA: Funny Paddymaniac!

MISS WONDERWRITE: No, not too much! Who composed *Menuet à l'Antique*? That is, Menuet G-dur, Opus 14, number 1? When you played it for the first time, Mozart's connoisseurs took it for an unknown Mozart's work. Chopin's lovers argued that it was a lost Chopin's composition discovered. They didn't want to believe that you wrote it. It was the most "Paderewski" composition of Paderewski. Inspired by Mozart, illuminated by Chopin, and yet totally original. Yours. I know it by heart. Can you play it for me?

PADEREWSKI: I can't.

MISS WONDERWRITE: Oh, there are so many recordings of it. You must have one, Maestro, somewhere.

♪ *She looks for a record, she finds it, she puts it into a pathephone and—when music starts—she speaks:*

The *Menuet* begins as if someone would test the smoothness of the dance floor with light touches of the foot, once and twice, once and twice. The theme is introduced in the first bars. It is simple, graceful, dancing, melodious, joyful... It greets and invites...

Then, an opposition arises between delicacy, moderation, and restraint and the temptation to sing loud, dance fast, and explode with unlimited vigor. Now! This is Paderewski! He could not miss an opportunity to run through the keys with wild abandonment and display his amazing technique. At the core part, the *Menuet* mutates into an, almost, Chopenian Mazurka. The echoes of Chopin wake the echoes of a Polish landscape in early autumn, here and there illuminated by rays of sun, fraught with the mysterious and unutterable Polish nostalgia. The country panorama seems to enlarge and embrace a ballroom in a castle, where airy shadows swirl. But suddenly the composition returns to a musical whisper. It poses clouded and enigmatic questions, repeats them and transforms, never answering with any certainty. We are left with the feeling of a mysterious ceremony in a palace of beauty, of which we are allowed only a glimpse as if through a half-open door... If a youngster could compose such a perfect work, an experienced artist will lead us to...

PADEREWSKI: That's that. A juvenile exercise.

MISS WONDERWRITE: No! A juvenile spark of a genius. *Menuet à l'Antique* was published first in Berlin in 1888 by Bote and Bock publishers.

PADEREWSKI: How do you know?

MISS WONDERWRITE: I know everything about you... You so often played it for an encore. I've heard it so many times... Now another surprise for you.

She pulls out from her bag an album with an inscription on the cover:

Ignacy Paderewski Ä Menuet à l'Antique

Theodore Pressler Publisher, Philadelphia, 1921.

A Homage to a Great Man and Great Artist.

Published in Memoriam of Maestro Paderewski's

Return to the World Concert Halls.

MISS WONDERWRITE: Theodore Pressler from Philadelphia published this *Menuet* again. In an enclosed letter Mr. Pressler begs you to accept this album hoping that he will be able to hand it over to you publicly after your next concert.

Paderewski browses the album.

PADEREWSKI: It's a well orchestrated plot. Steinway, Pressler, you... Anybody else?

MISS WONDERWRITE: Crowds. Crowds awaiting you! The whole music world is waiting for your return. We'll organize the first concert in Carnegie Hall in New York.

Miss Wonderwrite tries to put together the pieces of the poster scattered on the floor.

I beseech you, accept Steinway's proposal, listen favorably to Presslers' plea, trust me! You'll make a stunning success. You'll surpass all your past triumphs. You'll open a new chapter in the history of music. Please, agree, Master.

A pause.

PADEREWSKI: I won't agree.

MISS GLORIA: Good for California!

PADEREWSKI: In any case, not now. Please, understand, Miss Wonderwrite, that the decision to return to the life of a virtuoso would mean a return to the unbearably hard regimen of practice, which, by the way, this time, would not guarantee a success. Perhaps, it's too late? Perhaps I wouldn't be able to achieve full perfection of my fingers and absolute focus of my nerves, necessary to transform the potential energy of a performed piece into a real energy sent to the listeners? I don't know if I have enough strength to do it. I don't know if I have enough will power...

MISS WONDERWRITE: You do. I'm positive!

MISS GLORIA: I'm positive too. But we direct your will power to different goals. Fame of the Festival "Paderewski's Tempo Rubato in Paso Robles" will spread all over the world, as well as the reputation of the "Paderewski Zinfandel." Miss Wonderwrite, that poster is for nothing. Garbage! Mr. Paderewski does not need to travel anywhere to play and earn money. Money will come to him here. Of course, if he would like to play sometimes during the festival, or on a picnic, why not?

PADEREWSKI: Why not? Because, as I told you, the pianist must practice before playing in public. My fingers...

MISS GLORIA: Fingers? All right. I have an idea then. We will hire a pianist who will record your pieces on a mechanical piano—your know there are devices like that—and you, Mr. Paderewski, you will be sitting at the piano and pretending that you are playing while the mechanism does all the work. Nobody will know.

MISS WONDERWRITE: Barbarism!

PADEREWSKI: Great idea. You know how to do business, Miss Gloria.

MISS GLORIA: Yes! Together, we'll make millions. You and me.

MISS WONDERWRITE: And what about me? Or, rather, what about the music?

Knocking at the door.

PADEREWSKI: Come in, please.

Enters Fronczak.

FRONCZAK: May I?

PADEREWSKI: Please, you are welcomed. The ladies were about to leave. I've been waiting for you.

MISS WONDERWRITE: Before I go, please, maestro, give me your permission to cable Steinway.

PADEREWSKI: I permit you nothing.

MISS WONDERWRITE: Only that you're considering that November's concert? It's May now. You'd have half a year of...

PADEREWSKI: Half a year only? After eight years of non playing?

MISS WONDERWRITE: I beg you, master, in the name of music! In the name of love... of all music lovers.. Please, think it over...

PADEREWSKI: I shall think it over. This I can promise. But be patient. Good night.

MISS GLORIA: Till tomorrow, Mr. Paderewski. I called a press conference about our festival for ten in the morning. Oh, you didn't drink you coffee. Cold. I take it.

MISS WONDERWRITE: Till tomorrow. I'll not sleep a wink. May god Apollo watches over you. And Morpheus too. Good night.

Miss Wonderwrite and Miss Gloria exit.

PADEREWSKI: Doctor Fronczak! Thank you, my friend for coming from so far away, and thank you for waiting for such a long time.

FRONCZAK: Good to see you again, sir. Always good to see you. Shall we have a little exam, before we talk?

PADEREWSKI: The patient must obey the doctor. As you wish. But we can still talk.

FRONCZAK: Only a short routine.

During several following lines he examines Paderewski—he checks his pulse, listens to his breathing, looks into his eyes and mouth, examines his hands, and so on.

PADEREWSKI: How's Buffalo?

FRONCZAK: Always faithful to you. Buffalo has a plan for you, sir. In case you decide neither to return to Poland, nor to the piano.

PADEREWSKI: There's also a Californian option.

FRONCZAK: Mineral waters? They did so much good to you. A spa in Paso Robles

might be a medical hit.

PADEREWSKI: They prefer a bigger scale: wine and oil.

FRONCZAK: Are you considering it?

PADEREWSKI: It's tempting. Yet repulsive. There are also two retirement options. One in Switzerland, the other in Poland. But to retire one needs a capital to live on. My coffers are empty.

FRONCZAK: I understand. So, the choice is between music and politics?

PADEREWSKI: It looks that way. Music, paradoxically, would be a very difficult choice for a musician. I know best how difficult it would be. To run for Poland's presidencyÄnot any easier. Uncharted waters. May I be franc with you?

FRONCZAK: As always.

PADEREWSKI: I feel cornered.

FRONCZAK: I came to show you another way out.

PADEREWSKI: I can't guess.

FRONCZAK: What if you choose politics, but not in Poland?

PADEREWSKI: The presidency of the League of Nations?

FRONCZAK: It might be a position for you. But to run for it you must be a nominee of your country.

PADEREWSKI: The present Polish government would not like to have me in such position.

FRONCZAK: Thus, Geneva is a dead end. I know that you are contemplating Warsaw and I support that. I would be only too delighted if it works. But there's also Washington.

PADEREWSKI: What do you mean?

FRONCZAK: Here's the plan. You are the unquestionable leader of the American "Polonia." All Polish-Americans respect you, love you, believe in you. This can translate into about ten million votes.

PADEREWSKI: To run for the American presidency one has to be born in America.

FRONCZAK: Yes. But there's no such a condition for a senator.

PADEREWSKI: Explain it to me, please.

FRONCZAK: There are two states in the Union where Polish-Americans might make a difference. Illinois, with Chicago, and New York, with Buffalo. You would be a perfect candidate for New York's senator in the next year's elections. We have already organized a secret committee in Buffalo. Just a few people involved. Total confidentiality. We've evaluated the situation. There's a very good chance for your victory. You can count on all Polish votes and some Italian. Many Americans—Democrats, who remember your association with President Wilson, would vote for you too, and many Republicans as well, for they know how much President Warren Harding respects you. In addition, you could get many independents behind you. It wouldn't be necessary for you to join any political party. As in Poland, you could remain an independent. Of course, in politics as usual, you would be attacked. By the Germans, by the Irish, and by some Jews, who would like to denounce you for antisemitism, because of your loyalty to Roman Dmowski, considered, even if falsely, to be an antisemite. We would not debate Dmowski's views, but we would be able to dismiss any charges against you, proving they are completely unsubstantiated. Not only weren't you an antisemite, but you always spoke with respect about Jews. All together, you could be easly elected to the US Senate.

PADEREWSKI: From Buffalo?

FRONCZAK: From the state of New York. Of, course, you have to have the state's residency.

PADEREWSKI: I have my wine groves in California, and oil fields too.

FRONCZAK: Western New York also has wine plantations. And natural gas. You could make a trade. We can find you a fine estate on the Lake Erie shores or in the Orchard Park hilly forests. People are friendly and hospitable. So many Poles. Polish parishes, churches, schools. You'll love it.

PADREWSKI: And the weather? I heard bad things about Buffalo's weather? I shivered a few times there.

FRONCZAK: Myth. For you the Buffalo weather would be the closest to what you remember from Poland—four real, different

seasons, not that Californian eternal Spring, or Florida's unending Summer. Of course, you wouldn't be stuck in Buffalo. As a senator, you'd spend most of the time in Washington. In a warmer climate.

PADEREWSKI: You think that I'm worthy of the American people trust?

FRANCZAK: I do. I know that you wouldn't disappoint them as senator.

PADEREWSKI: I never thought about it before. But...yes... such an office could allow me to repay all that goodness which I, and Poland, have received from the American people. I could work for their good.

FRONCZAK: And you could help to improve the lives of millions of Polish-Americans, help them to fulfill their American dream. You could also continue influencing the fate of the Poles in the old country, by supporting Poland on the international scene, by sending economic help. You could mend many American problems too...

PADEREWSKI: So, instead of a Polish politician I should become an American one?

FRONCZAK: Not forgetting your Polish roots, of course, not betraying your love of Poland.

PADEREWSKI: But I still feel that my mission in Poland was left unfulfilled. Interrupted. In 1918, I returned to Poland simply to serve. Not to get power. Not to profit. I clashed with the conspiratorial ways of Piłsudski and the parliamentary tricks of Witos. I wanted to set a way in full sunlight—public, transparent, open. I dreamed about a Poland just, democratic, secure. Justice for all, regardless of nationality or race. Democratic, yet not divided along the party lines. Secure, because of the rule of law not the fear of the ruler. I gave Poland all I had—my name, my energy, my international connections and influences, along with my money. I kept nothing for myself. Including my music. With nothing I left. My name was defamed. My energy squandered. My influences disregarded. My money wasted. Who did it? Easy to manipulate crowds, biased journalists, parliamentary demagogues, military dumbheads. Things are bad in Poland now. Corruption of the political elites, scandals in corporations, disdain of the wealthy towards the poor, degeneration of the press. No end to the list... Am I not to return and confront the evil?

FRONCZAK: Your way of thinking is noble. Yet not realistic. You can't do politics without using political means...

PADEREWSKI: Tricks, hoax, deception, cynicism, lies?

FRONCZAK: Yes...

PADEREWSKI: So, what would be the difference between politics in Poland and in America?

FRONCZAK: We don't have paradise here either. Yet, we, the people of this country, ultimately decide our own destiny. Democracy is embedded here. In Poland—still to be implemented.

PADEREWSKI: Would I not be able to implement it there?

FRONCZAK: You could try. But you've tried already once and failed. You have to face that truth. Now, you could enter on the American political stage.

PADEREWSKI: I'm infinitely grateful to you for opening this door for me. Yet...

FRONCZAK: I understand. As in the old days—you have to think it over alone. By the way, I give you a clean bill of health. Your arthritis is under control. Your fourth finger seems to be healed.

PADEREWSKI: Thank you. You're a real friend. You understand me so well. Thank you again. We'll talk more tomorrow.

Fronczak exits.

PADEREWSKI: God knows that I wanted to serve Poland. Should I start serving America now? And what about serving music?

♪ *He goes to the piano. Opens the cover of the keyboard and plays one strong chord. A female's cry is heard behind the wall. Paderewski goes to the wall and knocks.*

PADEREWSKI: Helena? Helen? What happened? Do you need me, my dove?

Helena runs in.

PADEREWSKI: Helena, it's late. You can't sleep?

HELENA: How can I sleep if you are making noise all the time? Piano? People? What are you brooding about? What are you talking about? With these women? With those visitors? Some laughs? I heard them. I heard them laughing, how could I not hear, these walls are paper thin, these laughs are so awful.

What of? Of me? Of my dogs? Of my parrots? Of my hens? Why did you open that piano cover again? *She closes it.*

No more piano. No more concerts. Let's go to Switzerland. We'll settle on the Geneva Lake. The hens will feed us. The guest will entertain us. You'll have time for bridge, for the movies. We'll be at home, finally. Not in all these hotels, railway-cars, ship-cabins. What a strange fantasy—to sail with a piano to Australia, New Zealand, to play for the savages. The worst was the Royal Castle in Warsaw. Stairs too large, rooms to wide, doors to high, everywhere chambers not bedrooms, everyone enters and exits at their own will, and all run to you for decisions, for a signature, for advise, and, surely, for the money. Meetings, delegations, representatives, senators, ambassadors, ministers, beggars—get lost all or you!

And now these two women, oh, I know them, one is following you to every concert hall, sitting in the first row, clapping first. The other one is now crouching at the reception and screening all your moves, eves dropping on all your phone calls, bothering all your visitors. Both of them ready to jump into your bed. Don't stay any longer. Don't make me wait.

She exits.

A pause.

PADEREWSKI: Yes, Helena. Yes. I'm coming. Yes. We'll return to Switzerland. We'll watch from our bedroom window the pink dawns and the orange sunsets painted on the snows of Mt. Blanc. Clouds crowning Alpine peaks' laces. Fogs effacing the lake's silver plateau. Nobody and nothing will part us. Neither people, nor politics, not even music. Only death.

I remember, when we were still young, yes, we were young sometimes, hard to believe it now, it was before our marriage, you were the wife of... of somebody else... I came to see you in the evening... That is, I came to see my son, whom you so devoutly cared for, but he was already asleep. Your husband was not at home. I brought a poem written for you. I was ashamed to give it to you. I was afraid to stay with you. I suggested to you a walk.

We stopped at the river Seine's bank. Gas lamps reflections floated deep in the water. An accordion was heard from the shadows. Paris... thus an accordion... something so banal, yet immersing in such an overwhelming, nostalgic mood...

It was early May. Chestnuts' smell. I felt like kissing you, I put my hand on your shoulder, and you turned yourself to me... ready... and I knew that you wanted the same... and more... to return home, dismiss the servants... and I, instead of kissing you, I said, Helen, it's time to stop the time... and you looked at me... your big, radiant eyes... as two coins at the bottom of the Trevi fountain in Rome... when we threw them... under the moon... and you said, yes, it's time... For—I said—we've been together from ever, so, we have to stay together for ever... So, it happened. The time became timeless, transforming itself into a time of my love to you... Love—a total, undivided, all inclusive love of you, music, Poland.

Later, it started to divide. Music and Poland remained one chord. You became a dissonance. Then, music and Poland went two different ways, as the left and the right hand which do not play in tune. For a pianist—it's horrifying. So, you try to catch the harmony, but it get worse, it's no longer a "Tempo rubato," but a sheer cacophony, you desperately struggle to balance the tempos of the two hands, but you fail, fingers freeze...

Music, Poland, you... Which love? You'll not be the same as years ago. We'll not stop time. Now I know it. Poland from a dream-country transformed into its caricature. There's no way back. Music? Only music is eternal. It lasts. Its abyss is a way to the peak. Falling into its depth I could climb again.

Paderewski goes to the phone.

PADEREWSKI: Miss Gloria? Yes. I'm sorry, it's so late... But, would you be so kind to drop by to my apartment? Yes. Now. Is Miss Wonderwrite still there? Please, invite her too.

Sylvin has left, has he? Yes. Please, call Mr. Trojanowski and Doctor Fronczak. Please, tell them that I am very sorry, but I need them now. Oh, I almost forgot, please, wake up that visitor from Poland, that Mayor. No. Don't wake up my wife. She must be very tired. Yes. I'm waiting.

♪ *Paderewski goes to the pathephon and sets a record Chopin's "Etude No. 12 in C minor, Op. 10". He sits in an armchair and listens. One by one other characters come in. Paderewski invites them to sit. When the piece ends—he stands up.*

PADEREWSKI: Ladies and gentlemen, I'm very sorry to bother you so late. Yet, I need to share with you some thoughts... decisions... I did not want to delay.

Miss Gloria, you are so kind to play the role of my personal secretary, temporarily... Please, send a telegram to Sylvin, addressing it to Pan-American Express Railroad System, to be delivered in the train, please, put down "Warsaw's mission aborted. Stop. Continue travel to Europe. Stop. From Bremen go directly to Riond Bosson. Stop. Prepare the chateau for the coming of myself and my spouse next year. Stop. Detailed instructions will follow. Stop." My signature.

Miss Gloria, since I'm talking to you... Please, express my profound gratitude to the Paso Robles Town Council for their generous offers, and, please, accept my most sincere thanks for your kindness and help, yet, I will not be able to take advantage of them. My destiny is different. At the same time, I ask you to extend renting me the hotel for... yes... for the next six months, counting from today.

Mr. Plenipotentiary, I rescind my decision for drilling three new oil wells. Please, prepare all the necessary documents to put both the Ranch San Ignatio and the Ranch Santa Helena on the auction. Everything will go—land, wineries, wells, all. You'll start a search for the best bidders. The price must be fitting.

Mr. Mayor, I thank you for undertaking such a long journey. It was a pleasure to meet you. Mr. Plenipotentiary will pay you for all your travel expenses, in order not to expose the town of Ciężkowice to a financial loss.

I am utterly grateful for the invitation to Kąsna. Only God knows how much I loved, I love, that place. God knows that, and I want you to tell this to all of your fellow citizens, including children. You reminded me that once I invited the children from the neighboring villages to the circus in Tarnów.

Please, tell the children that I love them, that I long for them, but I can't come to see them. Nevertheless, to give them some proof of my love I send them a gift, a sum of one thousand dollars for the a trip to the circus. Mr. Plenipotentiary will write for you a check.

Doctor Fronczak, old, reliable, good friend, I am sorry, but I can't accept the offer from the Buffalo committee. I will not enter into the details of what kind of offer it was. A very generous one. Please, tell all Buffalonians that I cherish in my memory all the concerts I gave there. They were great audiences and hospitable people. I send them my most respectful greetings. I hope, I will be able to return to Buffalo again, in the future... Not for settling down, though... Yes...

Miss Wonderwrite, I thank you for you legation—in the name of music, the American music lovers, as well as the Steinway and the Pressler companies. Yet, it is not your prompting, but my own sense of duty which orders me to return to the concert halls. This will happen. Please, be so kind to inform Mr. Steinway that I accept his proposal. He may organize my concert in Carnegie Hall in New York. When? We may set the date. Today is May 21st, no, its already May 22nd. I need half a year for preparing myself. That will be half a year of twelve or more hours a day at the keyboard. You know that, do you? Yes, I pledge to appear in Carnegie Hall on November 22nd 1922.

You can give Mr. Steinway my initial repertoire, I'll confirm it soon. I'll begin with a Schubert, I'll play Chopin, of course, a waltz perhaps, some etudes, then List, probably "The Hungarian Rhapsody," what else, Wagner, "Liebestod," and my "Menuet," no doubt. I'll choose the encores later. You know that encores must be also practiced for months... Even if the virtuoso pretends that he is driven only by inspiration in choosing them...

What more? Please, inform Mr. Pressler that after the concert I shall be ready to accept his album, publicly. And you can inform the public that Padrewski returns.

Now, my dear friends, I'm not asking you for your opinions about my decision. I know that some of you are happy, some sad. I, myself, I have a heavy heart. I take this decision, as always, with a sense of duty. But believe me, this time it is not only the duty. It is love. Thank you, ladies and gentleman. Now, I'd like to be alone.

All present, who have been listening and reacting to Paderewski's words each on his/her own way—with a smile, a tear, a sigh, a joy, a sorrow—leave.

♪ Paderewski goes to the piano and touches the keys, as caressing them. He sets a record. It's again his "Menuet à l'Antique." He goes to the armchair, sits, and listens.

AN ALTERNATIVE EPILOGUE

Paderewski goes to the piano and opens the cover of the keyboard. He stands behind the piano. A Young Pianist enters. He sists at the keyboard. He starts performing Paderewski's "Menuete". Paderewski goes to the auditorium and sits in the front row. The Young Pianist performs the whole work. He stands up and bows to the public. Paderewski joins him. The rest of the cast joins.

THE END

≡ ∭ ≡

Paderewski at the piano in 1925 (National Digital Archives)

J. J. Paderewski (signature)

PADEREWSKI WRITINGS

Compiled by Maja Trochimczyk

Books and Editions

- *The Paderewski Memoirs*, by Ignacy Jan Paderewski and Mary Lawton. New York: Charles Scribner's Sons, 1938, 1939.
- *Pamiętniki,* ed. Mary Lawton. Polish trans. Wanda Lisowska and Teresa Mogilnicka. Kraków: PWM, 1986, 6th ed.
- *Pamiętniki: 1912-1932* [Memoirs: 1912-1932]. Edited by Mary Lawton. Translated, edited and introduced by Andrzej Piber. Kraków: Polskie Wydawnictwo Muzyczne, 1992.
- *The Paderewski memoirs, Part II, 1914-1932* by Ignace Jan Paderewski, eds. Mary Lawton and Christopher Onzol. Los Angeles: Paderewski Music Society, 2011.
- Ignacy Jan Paderewski, Halina Janowska (ed.), *Archiwum polityczne Ignacego Paderewskiego*. Instytut Historii (Polska Akademia Nauk) and Archiwum Akt Nowych w Warszawie. Published in Wrocław: Zakład Narodowy im. Ossolińskich, 1973-2007.
- *F. Chopin, Dzieła wszystkie*, [Complete Works]. Editor-in-Chief of the series. Kraków: PWM, 1949-61.
- *The Century Library of Music* vol. 1-20. New York: The Century Co., 1900-1902. Editor-in-Chief of the series. Co-edited by Fanny Morris Smith and Barnard Boekelman.

Articles

- "Korespondencje muzyczne z Berlina," [Musical correspondence from Berlin]. *Echo Muzyczne i Teatralne* no. 18 and 26 (1884); see also "O stylu narodowym w muzyce," reprint of one of these reports, *Muzyka* no. 3-4 (1932): 79.
- "*Konrad Wallenrod* Władysława Żeleńskiego" (recenzja) [review]. *Tygodnik Ilustrowany* no. 115 (1885): 175-6.

- "Antoni Rutkowski (Wspomnienie pośmiertne)." *Echo Muzyczne Teatralne i Artystyczne* (EMTA) no. 168 (18 December 1886): 543.
- "Impressions and Opinions." *Independent* vol. 52 (24 May 1900): 1234-1235.
- "What Good Piano Playing Calls For." *Ladies Home Journal* 24 (February 1907): 8.
- "Tempo rubato" in Henry Finck, *Success in Music and How It Is Won*. New York: Macmillan, 1909, 454-61 (in Polish in "Słowo Polskie" 1910 no. 49). Reprinted in *Polish Music Journal* vol. 4 no. 1 (summer 2001). Reprinted as "Poetic Piano Playing" in *Ladies' Home Journal* vol. 27 (March 1910): 17, 84. Reprinted as "Tempo rubato: The Best Way to Study the Piano." In *The Paderewski Paradox/Le paradoxe Paderewski*. Lincoln: Klavar Music Foundation, 1992.
- "Helpless Poland." *Independent* vol. 83 (9 August 1915): 192.
- "Paderewski Pleads for Food for Poland's Starving Millions." *Musical America* (16 October 1915).
- "Poland." Program of I.J. Paderewski: A Recital for the Polish Victims' Relief Fund, 10 October 1915.
- "W górę serca i oczy w górę! Apel Mistrza Paderewskiego," [Raise up your hearts and your eyes. An appeal by Paderewski], article published in May 1915 in *Jednodniówka of the Polish Roman-Catholic Union in Chicago*, chapter 15; reprinted in Józef Orłowski, ed. *Paderewski i Odbudowa Polski*, vol. 2. Chicago: The Stanek Press, 1940, 49-50.
- "Paderewski's Letter to Polish Organizations of 22 May 1915," published in Polish in Józef Orłowski, ed. *Paderewski i Odbudowa Polski,* vol. 2. Chicago: The Stanek Press, 1940, 66-67.
- "Independent Poland: Why the Ancient Democratic Nation Should be Resurrected." *World's Work* vol. 37 (December 1918): 173-179.
- "Future of Poland." *Living Age* vol. 301 (28 June 1919): 779-782.

- "Paderewski on Rhythm." *Etude* vol. 42 (December 1924): 882.
- "Chopin." *Etude* vol. 44 (February 1926): 95-96.
- "Nieznany list I. J. Paderewskiego" [Unknown Letter of Paderewski], to Bote und G. Bock of 1887. *Muzyka* no. 10 (1927): 508.
- Introduction to Charles Kellog, *Jadwiga, Poland's Great Queen,* New York, 1931.
- "O stylu narodowym w muzyce" [reprint of one of music reports of 1884] *Muzyka* no. 3-4, (1932): 79.
- *Poland and Peace*. London: Wishart & Co., 1933.
- "Musical Opinion," *Musical Digest* (October 1933), 9. Reprinted as "The Arts in the Wilderness," in *Polish Music Newsletter* vol. 7 no. 11 (November 2001).
- "Z mych wspomnień" *Muzyka* no. 4-6 (1933): 117-19 (trans. of an interview in *The Daily Mail* entitled "My Sixty Years of Music").
- Introduction to Henryk Opieński, ed. *Lettre de Chopin*, Paris, 1933.
- "Muzyka jedna jest istotnie żywą sztuką (wypowiedź)" [Music is really a live art. A statement] in "Trzy głosy o muzyce," [Three voices about music]. *Muzyka* no. 2 (1933): 3.
- "Poland's So-Called Corridor." *Foreign Affairs* vol. 11 (April 1933): 420-433.
- "Wizje przyszłości" [Visions of the future] *Muzyka* no. 1-2 (1936): 887.
- "Myśli uwagi, refleksje." [Thoughts, remarks, reflections]. *Muzyka* no. 2 (1934): 49-51.
- "Wizje przyszłości" [Visions of the future] *Muzyka* no. 1-2 (1936): 887.

Selected Speeches and Lectures

- "Chopin, mowa" in Obchód setnej rocznicy urodzin Chopina i Pierwszy Zjazd Muzyków Polskich we Lwowie, Lwów 1912, 195-202, see also: *Kompozytorzy polscy o Fryderyku Chopinie* (red. M. Tomaszewski), Kraków 1959,, 69-107. Published as *Chopin: A Discourse* in English trans. Laurence Alma-Tadema, London: Addlington, 1911. French trans. Laurence Alma-Tadema. New York, 1911. Reprint *Polish Music Journal* Vol. 4, No. 2 (winter 2001).
- "Paderewski's Speech." in "Paderewski as Orator and Pianist in San Francisco." *Musical Courier* (9 February 1915). Reprint *Polish Music Journal* Vol. 4 No. 1 (winter 2001).
- "Paderewski Pleads for Food for Poland's Starving Millions. Musical America (16 October 1915). Reprinted in *Polish Music Journal* 4 no. 1 (winter 2001).
- "Polska strażnikiem całej Europy! Polska Obrońcą Chrześcijaństwa!" Mowa Paderewskiego u stóp pomnika Kosciuszki (w dniu 15 Maja 1915) [Poland as the guardian of Europe! Poland as the Defender of Christianity. Paderewski's speech at the Kosciuszko Monument on 15 May 1915], published in Józef Orłowski, ed. *Paderewski i Odbudowa Polski*, vol. 2. Chicago: The Stanek Press, 1940, 54-55.
- *Poland Past and Present.* Address by Ignacy Jan Paderewski. New York, 1916.
- *Address* by Ignacy Jan Paderewski Delivered at the Polish Benefit Concert, Sunday Afternoon, February 5, 1916, at the Auditorium, Chicago, Illinois. New York: J. J. O'Brien & Son, 1916.
- "Mowa Mistrza I. J. Paderewskiego wygłoszona na wieczornicy żałobnej [...] z powodu śmierci Henryka Sienkiewicza" [Speech of Master Paderewski given on the memorial evening on the occasion of the death of Henryk Sienkiewicz], Chicago 1917; reprinted in Polish as "Mowa Paderewskiego ku Czci śp. Henryka Sienkiewicza" [Paderewski's Speech in Honor of H. Sienkiewicz], given at a

celebration organized by Wydział Narodowy in Chicago in November 1916), in Józef Orłowski, ed. *Paderewski i Odbudowa Polski*, vol. 2. Chicago: The Stanek Press, 1940, 173-175. Reprinted in English transl by Maria Piłatowicz in *Polish Music Journal* Vol. 4 No. 2 (winter 2001).
- "Paderewski w sprawie utworzenia Armii Kościuszkowskiej," [Paderewski about the creation of a Kościuszko Army], [Polish Falcons] speech at the Extraordinary Seym of the Sokolstwo, Pittsburgh, 8 April 1917, published in Józef Orłowski, ed. *Paderewski i Odbudowa Polski*, vol. 2. Chicago: The Stanek Press, 1940, 199-200.
- "W Stuletnią Rocznicę Zgonu Kościuszki," [On the hundredth anniversary of Kościuszko's death], speech of 17 October 1917, Chicago, Dexter Pavilion; published in Józef Orłowski, ed. Paderewski i Odbudowa Polski, vol. 2. Chicago: The Stanek Press, 1940, 213-216. English trans. by Maria Piłatowicz in *Polish Music Journal* Vol. 4 No. 2 (winter 2001).
- "W rocznicę zgonu T. Kościuszki w Jersey City, 25 Listopada 1917. Porywająca Mowa Paderewskiego." [On the anniversary of the death of Kosciuszko, in Jersey City, 25 November 1917. Sublime Speech by Paderewski], published in Józef Orłowski, ed. *Paderewski i Odbudowa Polski,* vol. 2. Chicago: The Stanek Press, 1940, 232-234.
- "Speech to the National Security League, 3 March 1918," in Józef Orłowski, ed. *Paderewski i Odbudowa Polski*, vol. 2. Chicago: The Stanek Press, 1940, English version 242-244; reprint *Polish Music Journal* 4 no. 2 (winter 2001). Polish transl J. Orłowski, 239-241.
- "Paderewski w odpowiedzi na mowę mayora Detroit," [Paderewski in response to the speech of the Mayor of Detroit], at the Wielki Seym Wychodzstwa Polskiego w Ameryce, [Great Seym of the Polish Emigration in America], Detroit, 26-30 August 1918. Published in Józef Orłowski, ed. *Paderewski i Odbudowa Polski,* vol. 2. Chicago: The Stanek Press, 1940, 279-281.

- "Przemówienie sejmowe z 20 II 1919 (na I posiedzeniu Sejmu Ustawodawczego)," [A Seym Speech of 20 February 1919, at the First Session of Seym], published in *Kurier Warszawski* no. 52 (21 II 1919). See also "Przemówienia sejmowe i in." (maszynopisy, odbitki rękopisów w zbiorach Ośrodka Paderewskiego), spis" [Seym Speeches and other ones; typescripts, copies of manuscripts in the collection of Paderewski Center: A Catalogue], in the Appendix of Małgorzata Perkowska-Waszek and Anne Strakacz-Appleton, eds. *Za kulisami wielkiej kariery. Paderewski w dziennikach i listach Sylwina i Anieli Strakaczów. 1936-1937.* [Behind the scenes of a great career: Paderewski in diaries and letters of Sylwin and Aniela Strakacz, 1936-1937]. Kraków: Musica Iagellonica, 1994.
- „O chwili bieżącej w Rzeczpospolitej" (Przemówienie sejmowe 12 XI 1919) [About the present moment of the Republic. A Speech at the Seym, 12 November 1919]. Kraków, 1919.
- *Discours prononcé* à Vevey, le 20 octobre 1924 a l'occasion de la translation des cendres de Henryk Sienkiewicz en Pologne. Lausanne 1925, see also "Mowa Mistrza..."
- "Remarks in Self-Defense," speech at a testimonial dinner of 1928, New York (originally untitled); in Part III of "Paderewski and the Tenth Anniversary of Poland's Independence (1928)" ed. Maja Trochimczyk, *Polish Music Journal* Vol. 4 No. 1 (Summer 2001).
- *Poland and Peace.* Garden City, 1932.
- "La Poméranie Polonaise," in *La Pologne et la Paix*, Warszawa 1933.
- *L'Allemagne et le Corridor polonais*, H. Strasburger. Paris: le Comité Polonais. n.d.
- "Buy a Share in America" [flyer, printout of a radio appeal], Washington D.C.: U.S. Treasury and U.S. Government Printing Office, 1941.

PADEREWSKI'S COMPOSITIONS

Compiled by Maja Trochimczyk

Notes

Paderewski's compositions have been published by
- Bote und G. Bock in Berlin, abbreviated to "B&B";
- 19th-century Polish periodical *Echo Muzyczne Teatralne and Artystyczne,* abbreviated to „EMTA" and its predecessors.
- *Utwory fortepianowe Ignacego Jana Paderewskiego* [Paderewski's Piano Works]. Ed. R. Smendzianka. vol. 1-8. Published as facsimile of early prints, Warsaw: Akademia Muzyczna im. F. Chopina, 1996.
- Series *Dzieła Wszystkie* [Complete Works] vol. 1-12 (ed. M. Perkowska-Waszek). Kraków: Musica Iagellonica, 1998 - 2007. Abbreviated to "CWP:. below. Eight volumes published so far. Vol. I, II, III i IV - *Utwory fortepianowe* (Piano Works); Vol. V - *Utwory Kameralne* (Chamber Music], Vol. VI – *Pieśni* (Songs); Vol. VIII - *Fantazja polska gis-moll, Op. 17* (Polish Fantasy in G-Sharp Minor); Vol. X *Uwertura Es- dur i Suita G-dur* (Overture in E-fat Major and Suite in G Major). Volumes in preparation: Vol. VII - *Koncert fortepianowy a-moll* (Piano Concerto in A Minor); Vol. IX - *Symfonia h-moll* (Symphony in B Minor); Vol. XI - Opera *Manru*; and Vol. XII - *Varia.*

≡ ∭ ≡

Music for and with Orchestra

Overture in E-flat Major, 1884. CWP, Vol. 10, 1997.

Suite in G Major for string orchestra, 1884. CWP, Vol. 10, 1997.

Symphony in B Minor., "Polonia," 1903-1909, Paris: Heugel et Cie, 1911.

Concerto in A Minor Op. 17 for piano and orchestra (dedicated to Theodore Leschetitzky), 1882-89. B&B, 1890.

Fantaisie polonaise sur des themes originaux in G-sharp Minor Op. 19 (dedicated to R. de Brancovan) 1891-93. B&B, 1895.

Manru. Lyric Drama in 3 acts to a libretto by Alfred Nossig, based on Józef Ignacy Kraszewski's novel, *Chata za wsią* [A hut beyond the village] 1893-1901, Published: Berlin Bote and Bock, 1901. Piano Reduction in Eng. Trans by Henry Krehbiel, New York: G. Schirmer, 1901. Premiered: Dresden, 29 May 1901.

Music for Piano Solo

Walc in F Major, ca. 1876, CWP, Vol. 4, 1997.

Impromptu in F Major, 1878/79 (dedicated to R. Stroblow), Wwa 1879 EM No. 11, CWP, Vol. 4, 1997.

Suite in E-flat Major, Op. 1 (dedicated to "F.[L.?]"), 1879, 4 mvts.:
    1. Preludium a Cappriccio in E-flat Major, Op. 1 No. 1;
    2. Menuetto in G Minor (published with changes as Minuetto in *Zwei Klavierstücke,* Op. 1, No. 2, B&B 1886),
    3. Romans in A-flat Major
    4. *Burleska* in E-flat Major

Trois morceaux, Op. 2 (dedicated to Wlasoff) 1880, Warszawa: Kruziński and Levi, 1881:
    1. *Gavotte* in E Minor
    2. *Mélodie* in C Major
    3. *Valse mélancolique* in A Major

Stara Suita, na trzy głosy [Old suite for 3 voices] Op. 3 (dedicated to A. Zarzycki), 1880/81, 4 mvts.; (dedication on manuscript: "for my wife" "for you"] 1880, published B&B, 1882:
1. Preludium in D Minor   2. Intermezzo in B-flat Major
3. Aria in F Major   4. Fugue in D Minor

Danses polonaises, Op. 5 (dedicated to Nathalie Janotha) 1881, Publ.: B&B, 1882:

    1. Krakowiak in E Major
    2. Mazurek in E Minor
    3. Krakowiak in B-flat Major

Introduction et toccata, Op. 6 (dedicated to P. Schlözer), 1881/82, Publ.: B&B 1884

Chants du voyageur, Op. 8 (dedicated to Helena Górska),1881-82, five mvts. Publ.: B&B, 1882:
    1. *Allegro agitato*   2. *Andantino*
    3. *Andantino grazioso*   4. *Andantino mistico*
    5. *Allegro giocoso*

Danses polonaises, Op. 9 (dedicated to H. Toeplitz), 1882 (No. 2-4) and 1884 (No. 1, 6), Publ.: B&B 1884:
    1. Krakowiak in F Major,   2. Mazurek in A Minor
    3. Mazurek in A Major   4. Mazurek in B Major
    5. Krakowiak in A Major   6. Polonez in B Major

Album de Mai. Scenes romantiques, Op. 10 (dedicated to A. Essipov) before January 1884, 5 mvts.; B&B 1884.
    1. *Au soir*   2. *Chant d'amour*   3. Scherzino
    4. Barcarola   5. *Caprice-valse*

Powódź [Flood] in A Minor, 1884, publ. in *Na pomoc* [Help!], an occasional brochure, Warsaw, 1884. CWP, Vol. 4, 1997.

Intermezzo in C Minor, 1882 (part of an unfinished piano sonata), EMTA No. 77, 89, 1885; CWP Vol. 4, 1997.

Variations et fugue sur un theme original in A Minor Op. 11 (dedicated to E. d'Albert), 1882/3 and 1884, B&B 1885.

Album tatrzańskie [The Tatra Album], Op. 12 (4 mvts.), 1883 (No. 1-3), 1884 (No. 4).
    1. *Allegro comodo* (Publ.: Warsaw, 1883 EMTA No. 1)
    2. *Andantino grazioso*
    3. *Maestoso, vivace*
    4. *Allegro poco moderato,* Publ.:1884 EMTA No. 314, 41, 51

Tatra Album. Tänze und Lieder des polnischen Volkes aus Zakopane [Polish folk dances and songs from Zakopane, arranged by the composer for 4 hands], (dedicated to Tytus Chałubiński) 1884, 6 mvts.; published Berlin: Ries und Erler, 1884

    Part I:
    1. *Allegro con brio.* 2. *Andantino,* 3. *Allegro con moto;*
    Part 2:
    4. *Allegro maestoso,* 5. *Allegretto* 6. *Allegro ma non troppo,*

Suite in E-flat Major (unfinished; movements published separately):
    1. Toccata, 1886-87 (published as Op. 16)
    2. Preludium. 1885 (published as Op. 1, No. 1)
    3. Scherzo [missing]
    4. Romans. 1885/86 (published *Melodia* or *Legenda* Op. 16)
    5. Intermezzo. 1886 (published as Op. 14, Part 2, No. 2)
    6. Variations and Finale. 1885-87 (publ Op. 16, No. 3 & Op. 23)

Zwei Klavierstücke Op. 1 (dedicated to A. Rutkowski):
    1. *Praeludium et capriccio* in E-flat Major, 1885,
    2. *Minuetto* in G Minor 1879, B&B 1886;

Humoresques de concert, Op. 14 (dedicated to A. Essipov), 6 works:
Cahier 1, à l'antique, B&B, June 1887:
    1. Minuet in G Major (before 8 Nov. 1886)
    2. Sarabande in B Minor (Jan. 1887)
    3. *Caprice* (genre Scarlatti) in G Major (Jan. 1887)
Cahier 2, moderne. B&B, Oct. 1887:
    4. *Burlesque* in F Major (ca. 1887)
    5. *Intermezzo polacco* in C Minor (1885/86)
    6. *Cracovienne fantastique* in B Major (Nov. 1886, Publ.: Warsaw. 1887. EMTA No. 171, without opus, dedicated to A. Michałowski);

Dans le désert. l. *Tableau musical en forme d'une toccata* in E-flat Major Op. 15 (dedicated to A. Essipov, prob. Anna Yesipova, Russian pianist) 1886-87, published B&B, 1887.

Miscellanea. Série de morceaux Op. 16, 7 works, editions: No. 1-3, B&B ca. 1888, No. 1-4, ca. 1892, No. 5, ca. 1895, Op. 16, ca. 1895-96:
> 1. *Légende* No. 1 in A-flat Major, written in 1886 or 1888 (dedicated to C. Scheurer-Kästner),
> 2. *Mélodie* in G-flat Major, 1885 (dedicated to M. Trélat),
> 3. *Thème varié* in A Major, 1885-87 (dedicated to A. Weber-Schlumberger),
> 4. Nocturne in B Major, ca. 1890-92 (dedicated to R. de Brancovan),
> 5. *Légende* No. 2 in A Major, ca. 1894 (dedicated to H. Bibesco), Publ.: New York, Nov. 2, 1894 in *The Strand Magazine.*
> 6. *Un moment musical,* 1891, Published: New York, 2 Oct. 1891 *The New York Herald*
> 7. Minuet in A Major, 1890-1896. Publ.: London, Wilcocks, ca. 1896; 8. *Canzone. Chant sans paroles*, ca. 1890-1903, Publ.: B&B, ca. 1907, CWP vol. 4 1997.

Mazurka in G Major 1896, facsimile, Publ.: Philadelphia 1896 in *Ladies' Home Journal.* CWP, Vol. 4, 1997.

Miniatura in E-flat Major, no date. Publ.: CWP, Vol. 4, 1997. Sonate pour piano in E-flat Minor Op. 21, 1887 and 1903 (dedicated to Austrian Prince Karol Stefan), Publ.: B&B, ca. 1906, CWP, Vol. 3, 2000.

Variations et fugue sur un theme original in E-flat Minor, Op. 23, 1885 and 1903 (dedicated to W. Adlington), Publ.: B&B, no date. ca. 1906, CWP, Vol. 3, 2000.

Music for Chamber Ensembles

Piece in F Major for violin and piano (dedicated to Józef Ignacy Kraszewski), 1878.
Romance in A Major for violin and piano, Op. 7, ca. 1881-82 (dedicated to Władysław Górski).
Sonata in A Minor, Op. 13, for violin and piano, composed in January to April, 1885 (dedicated to Pablo de Sarasate), pub. B&B, 1886.
Variations and Fugue for String Quartet, 1882; 3 sketches, 1882, 1884, 1887 (incomplete).
Ćwiczenia [Excercises] for wind ensemble, 1884 (unpublished).

Songs and Choral Music

Vier Lieder, Op. 7, to texts by Adam Asnyk 1882-85 (dedicated to Adam Asnyk), Publ.: B&B, ca. 1888:
    1. *Gdy ostatnia róża zwiędła* [when the last rose withers]
    2. *Siwy koniu* [Grey horse]
    3. *Szumi w gaju brzezina* [The birch rustles in the grove]
    4. *Chłopca mego mi zabrali* [They took my boy away from me]

Konwalijka [Lily of the valley] ("Nie będę ci rwała"...[I will not pluck you...] to words of A. Asnyk [Lily of the valley Op. 7, No. 5, 1882, not included in the edition by B&B)

Six Songs Op. 18 to texts by Adam Mickiewicz 1887-93 (dedicated to Władysław. Mickiewicz), Publ.: B&B 1893:
    1. *Polały się łzy* [The tears flowed]
    2. *Idę ja Niemnem* [and go along Niemen] (Dudziarz)
    3. *Moja pieszczotka* [My darling]
    4. *Nad wodą wielką* [Upon the great water]
5. *Tylem wytrwał* [I have endured so much]
6. *Gdybym się zmienił* [If and should change]

Dans la forêt to a text by Theodore Gautier, ca. 1896 (dedicated to Maurel), New York, G. Schirmer, 1896

Douze Mélodies sur des Poésies de Catulle Mendès, Op. 22, to poetry of C. Mendès, 1903 (dedicated to M. Trélat), Paris, Heugel et Cie, ca. 1904 (Published in German in 1911):

1. *Dans la forêt*
2. *Ton coeur est d'or pur*
3. *Le ciel est très bas*
4. *Naguère*
5. *Un jeune pâtre*
6. *Elle marche d'un pas distrait*
7. *La nonne*
8. *Viduité*
9. *Lune froide*
10. *Querelleuse*
11. *L'Amour fatal*
12. *L'Ennemie;*

Hej, Orle Biały! Hymn bojowy poświęcony Armii Polskiej w Ameryce. [Hey, White Eagle. Military Anthem dedicated to the Polish Army in America], to a text by the composer; song for male chorus and piano or wind ensemble. 1917 New York, published in 1918; also published: Songs CWP vol. VI, 2001. Text reprinted and translated into English by Maja Trochimczyk in Trochimczyk, "Master of Harmonies or Poland's Savior? Paderewski in Poetry," *Polish Music Journal* 4 no. 1 (summer 2001).

PADEREWSKI ARCHIVES AND MUSEA

List Compiled by Maja Trochimczyk

- *Archiwum Ignacego Jana Paderewskiego* (Paderewski Archive) in Archiwum Akt Nowych (Archives of New Records), Warsaw. Archival collections from 1880 to 1941.

- *Ignacy Jan Paderewski's Personal Library* at the Ośrodek Dokumentacji Muzyki Polskiej XIX I XX wieku im. I. J. Paderewskiego. Jagiellonian University, Institute of Musicology, Kraków, Poland.

- *The Paderewski Room.* Polish Museum of America, Chicago.

- *Paderewski Archive – The Paso Robles Collection.* Polish Music Center, University of Southern California, Los Angeles. Donated by Henry Blythe III.

- Musée Paderewski, Le Château, Rue du Château, 1110 Morges, paderewski-morges.ch (near his former estate in Riond Bosson).

- Muzeum Wychodźstwa Polskiego im. Ignacego Jana Paderewskiego w Warszawie. Oddział Muzeum Łazienki Królewskie w Warszawie, ul. Agrykola 1, 00-460 Warszawa, Poland, www.lazienki.ueu.pl.

- Paderewski Centre/Centrum Paderewskiego w Kąśnej Dolnej. Kąśna Dolna 17 | 33-190 Ciężkowice, Poland. centrumpaderewskiego,pl.

SELECTED BOOKS AND STUDIES ABOUT PADEREWSKI

Compiled by Maja Trochimczyk

Andress, Bart. *Ignace Jan Paderewski: Artist, Humanitarian, Statesman: A Digest of Material for Speakers, Writers and Campaign Workers.* New York: Paderewski Fund for Polish Relief, 1940 or 1941.

Baughan, :Edward Algernon. *Ignaz Jan Paderewski.* London, New York: J. Lane Co., 1940, 3nd ed.

Biskupski, Mieczysław B. 'Paderewki as Leader of American Polonia, 1914-1918,' Polish American Studies 43:1 (1986), 37-56.

Biskupski, M. B. "Paderewski, Polish Politics, and the Battle of Warsaw, 1920." *Slavic Review*, Vol. 46 (1987), 503.

Biskupski, M. B. "The Origins Of The Paderewski Government In 1919: A Reconsideration in Light of New Evidence." *The Polish Review*, Vol. 33 (1988), 157.

Biskupski, M. B. „Wilson, Paderewski, and the Polish Question, 1914-1921: Eugene Kusielewicz's Historical Works." *Polish American Studies*, Vol. 56, 1999, 89.

Borland, Andrew. *Paderewski, Polish Pianist and President.* Kilmarnock: John Ritchie, 19--.

Braun, Kazimierz. *Dzieci Paderewskiego. Paderewski's children. Paderewski wraca. Paderewski returns. Dwa dramaty. Two dramas.* Warsaw: Instytut Dziedzictwa Myśli Narodowej im. Romana Dmowskiego i Ignacego J. Paderewskiego, 2021.

Braun Kazimierz. *Dramaty Zebrane. Collected Plays. Tom 4. Volume 4. Teatr Pamięci. Theater of Memory* (two plays about Paderewski in Polish and English). Los Angeles: Moonrise Press, 2025.

Drozdowski, Marian Marek. *Ignacy Jan Paderewski: pianista, kompozytor, mąż stanu.* Warszawa Wydawnictwo DiG, 2001.

Drozdowski, Marian Marek. *Tradycja Kościuszkowska w życiu i twórczości Ignacego Jana Paderewskiego.* Polska Fundacja Kościuszkowska, 1991.

Cartwright, Jim. *Immortal Performances Discographic Data: No. 6, Ignace Jan Paderewski Recordings.* Austin: J. Cartwright, 1978.

Ciepliński, Jan. *Ignacy Jan Paderewski (w setną rocznicę urodzin).* Wykonano w drukarni Spółki Wydawn. Czas, New York, 1960.

Dobrzanski, Slawomir. "From Paderewski to Penderecki: The Polish Musician in Pennsylvania." *The Polish Review*, Vol. 63 No. 1, January 2018, 99.

Dodson, Alan. "Metrical Dissonance and Directed Motion in Paderewski's Recordings of Chopin's Mazurkas." *Journal of Music Theory*, Vol. 53 (2009), 57.

Dulęba, Władysław, Zofia Sokołowska, and Wiktor Litwinski. *Paderewski.* New York: Kościuszko Foundation, 1979.

Dziadek, Magdalena, Michał Jaczyński, Justyna Kica. "The Grand Piano of Ignacy Jan Paderewski in Cartoons." *Fontes Artis Musicae*, 70, 2023L 34.

Finck, Henry T. *Paderewski and His Art.* New York: Wittingham and Atterton, 1892.

Giron, Simone. *Tajemnica testamentu Paderewskiego* [Mystery of Paderewski's Last Will]. Kraków: PWM, 1996.

Hoskins, Janina W. *Ignacy Jan Paderewski, 1860-1941: A Viographical Sketch and a selective list of reading materials.* MLibrary, Prepared for Publishing by HP, Ann Arbor, 2011.

Howard, Lord of Penrith. "Paderewski: Musician, Patriot, Statesman." *Foreign Affairs*, Vol. 14, No. 1 (1936), 309.

Jenner, Aleksander. "The 'Paderewski Edition' of Chopin's Works." *Musicus*, Vol. 32, No. 1 (January 2004), 128.

Jezierski, Bronislas A. "Paderewski and the Treaty of Versailles." *Polish American Studies*, 11 (1954), 42.

Kellog, Charlotte. *Paderewski*. New York: Viking Press, 1956.

Kędra, Władysław. *Ignacy Paderewski*. Warsaw: Czytelnik, 1948.

Kozubek, Lidia. *Manru Ignacego Jana Paderewskiego*. Katowice: Wydawnictwo Unia, 2001.

Krehbiel, Henry Edward. *Analytical Notes on M. Paderewski's Programmes*. New York: [No publisher], 1899.

The Kościuszko Foundation. *To Ignace Jan Paderewski, Artist, Patriot, Humanitarian*. New York: The Kościuszko Foundation, 1928.

Krzyżanowski, Jerzy R. *Henryk Sienkiewicz and Ignacy Paderewski*. New York: The Polish Institute of Arts and Sciences in America, 1970.

Kulisiewicz, Eugene. "Paderewski and Wilson's Speech to the Senate, January 22, 1917." *Polish American Studies*, Vol. 13 (1956), 65.

Landau, Rom. *Paderewski*. London: Ivor Nicholson and Watson, 1934.

Lisandrelli, Elaine. *Ignacy Jan Paderewski: Polish Pianist and Patriot*. Morgan Reynolds Publishing, January 1999, biography for youth.

Lorkowska Halina. *Ignace Jan Paderewski: The Man and His Work*. Beata Brodniewicz, Transl., Poznań: I.J. Paderewski Academy of Music, 2015.

Majewska, Magdalena. *Paderewski*. Brief biography in English transl. by Magdalena Majewska. Kraków: PWM, 2025.

Majewska, Magdalena. *Paderewski.* In Polish. Kraków: PWM, 2025.

Marcus, Kenneth, H. "Modjeska, Paderewski, and the California Landscape." *Southern California Quarterly,* 100 (April 2018), 69.

Marczewska-Zagdańska, Hanna and Janina Dorosz, 'Wilson – Paderewski – Masaryk: Their Visions of Independence and Conceptions of how to Organize Europe.' *Acta Poloniae Historica* 73 (1996), 55–69.

McGinty, Brian. *Paderewski at Paso Robles.* Scottsdale, AZ: Overland Books, 2004.

Michell (n.n). *The Brighton Album.* Untitled album of press clippings, photos, ephemeral documents, and writings, 1890-1914. Unpublished.

Modelski, I. *Ignacy Paderewski w walce o wielką Polskę.* Drukiem Przewodnika Katolickiego, New Britain, Conn., 1933.

Modjeska, Helena (Helena Modrzejewska). *Memories and Impressions of Helena Modjeska: An Autobiography.* New York: McMillan, 1910.

Moran, Michael. *The Pocket Paderewski: The Beguiling Life Of The Australian Concert Pianist Edward Cahill.* Melbourne: Australian Scholarly, 2016.

Orłowski, Józef, ed. *Ignacy Jan Paderewski i odbudowa Polski.* Chicago: H.T. Beckert, Vol. 1, 1939, Vol. 2, 1940.

Paderewska, Helena. *Paderewski: The Struggle for Polish Independence (1910–1920),* Ilias Chrissochoidis, ed. Stanford: Stanford University Press, 2015.

Paderewski: Twentieth American Tour Souvenir Program. Los Angeles: J. Paul Huston for Peter D. Conley, 1939.

The Paderewski Foundation. *Ignacy Jan Paderewski, 1860-1941; memorial album.* New York: The Paderewski Foundation, 1953.

The Paderewski Foundation. *Paderewski Notes*. A magazine of The Paderewski Foundation in New York, no. 1, 1976.

Paderewski, Józef. *Wieniec grunwaldzki z 1910-go roku : wydawnictwo historyczne, pamiątkowe ilustrowane: zbiór aktów i dokumentów historycznych z 1910 r. ku uczczeniu 500 letniej rocznicy wiekopmnego zwycięztwa Polaków nad Krzyżakami*. Kraków: Skład Główny w Księgarni Gebethnera i Spółki, 1910.

Paja-Stach, Jadwiga. *Polish music from Paderewski to Penderecki*. English transl. Cara Emily Thornton. Krakow: Musica Iagellonica, 2010.

Perkowska, Małgorzata. *Diariusz koncertowy Ignacego Jana Paderewskiego*. Kraków Polskie Wydawnictwo Muzyczne, 1990.

Perkowska-Waszek, Małgorzata. *Ignacy Jan Paderewski (1860-1941) : portrait of man, artist, and statesman : an exhibition on the 50th anniversary of the artist's death : Museum of Jagiellonian University--Collegium Maius, 31 May-23 June 1991*. Kraków: The Museum, 1991.

Perkowska-Waszek, Małgorzata. *Paderewski i jego twórczość : dzieje utworów i rys osobowości kompozytora*. Kraków: Musica Iagellonica, 2010.

Phillips, Charles. *Paderewski: The Story of a Modern Immortal*. New York, McMillan, 1933.

Piber, Andrzej. *Droga do sławy: Ignacy Jan Paderewski w latach 1860-1902* [Way to fame: Ignacy Jan Paderewski in the years 1860-1902] Warsaw: PIW, 1982.

Poniatowska, Irena. *Chopin w poezji*. Warsaw: NIFC, 2020.

Prazmowska, Anita. *Ignacy Paderewski. Poland*. Makers of the Modern World. London: Haus Publishing, 2010.

Prazmowska, Anita and Françoise Stonborough. *Ignace Paderewski et la renaissance de la Pologne en 1919*. Lausanne: Les Editions Noir sur Blanc, 2014.

Pylee, M.V. *Annual Symposium 1962: Paderewski Scholars in India*. New Delhi: Paderewski Foundation, 1963.

Rich, Ruth Anne. "Paderewski: America's Million-Dollar Pianist." *American Music Teacher*, 30, 1981, 44.

Richards, Mrs. George S. *Ignace Jan Paderewski, world's greatest pianist*. Duluth, Minn., n.p., 1924.

Roman, Kazimierz and Haag Czekaj. *Ignacy Jan Paderewski: album Międzynarodowego Towarzystwa Muzyki Polskiej im. Ingacego Jana Paderewskiego w Warszawie*. Warsaw and Basel: Die Internationale Vereinigung-Paderewski zur Forderung der Polnichen Musik, Warszawa, Basel, Switzerland, 2010.

Sieradz, Małgorzata. „Riond-Bosson i Ignacy Jan Paderewski w relacji Ludwika Bronarskiego." *Muzyka*, 69, 2024.

Sitarz, Andrzej and Wojciech Marchwica. *Warsztat kompozytorski, wykonawstwo i koncepcje polityczne Ignacego Jana Paderewskiego* [Composers workshop: Performance and political conceptions of I. J. Paderewski]. Conference proceedings from Jagiellonian, U., 1991. Kraków: Musica Iagellonica, 1991.

Steinway & Sons. *Paderewski*. Booklet published ca. 1895 by piano-maker Steinway & Sons.

Stevenson, Ronald and Harriette Brower. *The Paderewski paradox = Le paradoxe Paderewski*. Lincoln [England]: Klavar Music Foundation 1992.

Strakacz, Aniela. *Paderewski as I Knew Him*. Trans. Halina Chylewska. New Brunswick: Rutgers University Press, 1949.

Towarzystwo Muzyczne im I. J. Paderewskiego w Bydgoszczy. *Rok Ignacego Jana Paderewskiego*. Bydgoszcz: Towarzystwo Muzyczne im. Ignacego Jana Paderewskiego w Bydgoszczy, 2001.

Trochimczyk, Maja. "Paderewski in Poetry: Master of Harmonies or Poland's Savior?" in "Paderewski and Polish Emigres in America;" special issue of the *Polish Music Journal* 4, no. 1 (Summer 2001).

Trochimczyk, Maja, ed. 'Paderewski and the Tenth Anniversary of Poland's Independence (1928),' in "Paderewski – Lectures and Documents," *Polish Music Journal* 4, No. 1 (2001), online.

Trochimczyk, Maja. "Searching for Poland's Soul: Paderewski and Szymanowski in the Tatras," in *A Romantic Century in Polish Music,* Maja Trochimczyk, ed., Moonrise Press, 2009, 179-219.

Trochimczyk, Maja. "An Archangel at the Piano: Paderewski's Image and his Female Audience." *Polish American Studies* 67, no. 1 (Spring 2010): 5-44.

Trochimczyk, Maja. "Romantic, Sublime, Heroic, Immortal – Paderewski in American and English Poetry" a chapter forthcoming in Stephen Downes, ed. *Modern Constructions of "Polish" Music outside of Poland*, 2025.

Trochimczyk, Maja, ed. *Polish Music Journal*. Online, peer-reviewed journal for research in Polish music (1998-2003). Founder and Editor. Two issues dedicated to Paderewski. Vol. 4, No. 1 (2001, "Paderewski and Polish Emigres in America"), and Vol. 4, No. 2 (2001, "The Unknown Paderewski").

Wapiński, Roman. *Ignacy Paderewski*. Wrocław, 1999.

Zamoyski, Adam. *Paderewski*. New York, 1982.

Żebrowski, Marek. *Celebrating Chopin and Paderewski*. Warsaw: Ministry of Foreign Affairs, Department of Public and Cultural Diplomacy, 2010.

Żebrowski, Marek. *Paderewski in California*. Toruń: Tumult Foundation, 2009.

www.ingramcontent.com/pod-product-compliance
Lightning Source LLC
Chambersburg PA
CBHW062045220426
43662CB00010B/1653